Compquest Volume 1

Compquest Volume 1

In Search of Computer Literacy

Jay S. Lurie

Writers Club Press
San Jose New York Lincoln Shanghai

Compquest Volume 1
In Search of Computer Literacy

Writers Club Press
an imprint of iUniverse.com, Inc.

For information address:
iUniverse.com, Inc.
5220 S 16th, Ste. 200
Lincoln, NE 68512
www.iuniverse.com

ISBN: 0-595-17466-3

Printed in the United States of America

I dedicate this book to my daughter, Haley.

Table of Contents

*Windows tips & tricks

List of Illustrations

Chapter 9.5

Chapter 10

Chapter 11

Chapter 12

Chapter 13

Chapter 14

Chapter 15

Foreword

My name is Jay, and I'll be your tour guide throughout this book as we make our way through a computer system and the Internet. I started toying with computers circa 1980. I had a feeling at the time that I should make it my business to learn these machines, but I really didn't. I mean for the next 20 years I used computers on and off. I primarily used IBM compatibles (PCs), but I was into Apple Macintosh computers for a couple of years in that 20-year period. I know what it's like to be a beginner because I had a renewed interest in computers just a few years ago. At that point, I had lost touch with the nuances of these machines. Writing is my forte, and although typewriters have been outdated for quite sometime, all I really needed a computer for was word processing. I kind of lost touch with all the tips & tricks for computers. Although I have spent an inordinate amount of time on these machines, I would start the computer, open my word processor, do my work, and then shut down. I never really learned anything more about computers than I already knew after the first few years of toying with them.

I was Vice President of a small corporation. Computers weren't that important to our small company. I did some basic tasks on a computer and that's it. It was in the early to mid '90s when I held that position—the time before computers really became imperative in the business world—especially for a small business.

I obtained a less prestigious job as a computer technician. At that time, I was out of the high-tech loop because of the previously mentioned reasons. That's why I think that I can relate to novices and write some advice that relays what most beginners really need or want to know. Even before my techie days, I did know the steadfast information about computers such as what RAM and ROM are; things of that nature haven't ever changed about computers. As a technician, I learned a lot by on the job training (OJT), like we called it in the military, and I looked at the job as a learning experience. It was uptraining for computers that I had lost touch with in recent years. And I always kept in mind that I was getting paid to learn. I wasn't getting paid much mind you, but I had a little money saved up, so I could afford to work for less than I was accustomed to for the computer education.

After several years of troubleshooting systems via the telephone, I finally felt that I was ready to write a book such as this one. I could relate to beginners, I knew enough to know what's important to mention and what isn't, and I knew what novices want to know most often after talking to around 50,000 people over the years—most of them brand new or fairly new to computers. For these reasons I felt that I was not only qualified to write a book like this, but I was an ideal candidate.

It is impossible to please everybody in any given situation. However, I wrote this book with 2 main objectives in mind: 1) I wanted to write a tutorial book that had a different perspective than most books of this type—more personable, more direct, more explanatory. 2) I intended to write a book that would appeal to the largest possible audience of novice computer users. I truly hope that I did a good job of meeting my objectives.

A secondary objective of this work is to gain a little fame. Fortune really wasn't a major factor or motivation for me to write this book. Of course, if that came as a by-product, it would be nice, but it certainly wouldn't be expected. I guess a goal of mine for many years has been to be able to walk into a bookstore and see a book with my name on it. More importantly, and perhaps a 3rd main objective, was simply to write a book that would actually tell someone that knows nothing about a computer how to use one—in plain English language. I really do enjoy helping people with their computers; that's one thing that kept me at my tech support job for as long as I had been there. Moreover, I intended to write a book that I think everyone should read that just got a computer for the first time. I think that there should be some required reading before a person operates a computer. If not this book, then everyone that doesn't know anything about a computer should read some book or literature along these lines.

The reason why required reading is a good idea is that a computer is not like a toaster where you can just pitch the instructions and start making toast. It's not a VCR where you can just accept the blinking clock that reads 12:00 and go on and watch movies. A computer is one of the situations where you really need to read the instruction manual. But the manual won't tell you that much about the real world applications or situations that you may run into. It won't tell you about the Internet and that sort of thing. That's where a book like this comes in. A computer is so profound, and there is such an incredible amount of data to know about computers and the Internet that this entire book doesn't even begin to come close to covering it all—but it's a good start. The book isn't meant to be an end all or be all to using a computer but merely a foundation or a stepping stone on your way to becoming an expert. If all that you ever want to do is to learn enough to operate your computer efficiently and fairly comfortably, then I really think this is the book for you. The reason why this book appeals to the largest audience is that it will both serve as a stepping stone for those who want to become a computer guru, and it will serve as a decent standalone tutorial if you're a person who really doesn't care in the least bit how a computer works but you need to use one for one reason or another. You owe it to yourself to get a little knowledge on the subject if you are going to use a computer, either voluntarily or involuntarily, for any reason. You will be a lot less frustrated and a lot more productive if you gain a decent element of understanding on the subject of computers. If you read this entire book, and retain most of it, there is no doubt in my mind that you will be clicking around the Internet like an expert in just a short while.

Now that I've introduced myself, I am anxious to get started, as I'm sure you are. I really enjoyed writing this book. Interestingly, I wrote the Foreword after I completed everything else—even the Glossary! That is congruent with my intention to make this a little different then a traditional tutorial book. I tried to make it a book with a twist; I intentionally deviated from the norm in some ways to make it interesting. If my readers enjoy reading this book at least half as much as I enjoyed writing it, I will feel like I have done a good job.

Preface

I believe that you can be comfortable on your computer in just a short time like a month. You probably won't be an expert, but at least you can have an understanding of why things are the way they are with your computer. There are literally thousands of things you may not even realize that you can do on a computer. I have written this book in a manner so that if you read and digest the information, it will increase your productivity on your computer and minimize your frustration. If you are like me, you never have enough time either, so I tried to make this book as succinct as possible without omitting the really important information. If you want to go on to become a computer expert (or close to one), there are plenty of books that go into painful detail on the subject. This book is not one of them. Rather, I have attempted to engineer it so that it would appeal to the widest range of computer novices as possible; it is a good accompaniment to other books of its type such as *Windows for Dummies* or *The Internet for Dummies*. If you apply yourself, you could very well be a computer expert in maybe 6 months from where you are now even if you are starting from ground zero. This book is simply a good place to start.

I have taken technical support calls for a large Internet service provider (ISP) for years, and I talked to many people that knew absolutely nothing about a computer—believe me! If you are one of these people, then don't worry. You are not alone. But the point is that you have to start somewhere, and I had to start somewhere when writing this book so I started out in simple terms. If you know the very basics and know how to use a mouse, but you know that you have some more to learn, you may want to skip down to one of the chapters a little bit down the road. In general, the higher the number of the chapter the more advanced the lesson is.

What really sparked the creation of this book is that I recognized the need for some basic information about a computer and even specific instructions for beginner to intermediate functions that you can perform on a computer. Lots of people crave this information, and they are curious and inquisitive. I know because I have talked to people that had a dozen or so questions in one phone call. I'm pretty sure that some people had written these down on a notepad before making the call to tech support. So hopefully the following tutorials will answer a lot of your frequently asked questions and maybe some of your not-so-frequently asked questions. It is hard to strike a happy medium between a long-winded book and one that's just too terse. I made a concerted effort to land in this gray area; to provide enough information without going overboard. Although it may seem like it is a bit loquacious, I did cut a lot out of it. What challenged me the most when writing this book was that I had to streamline it without watering it down or sacrificing pertinent information.

An interesting phenomena that I have noticed follows:

A lot of people seem to take pride in not understanding computers. If you are, or plan to be, in the business world, you'd better learn them. About 80% of jobs these days require some computer knowledge or working on a computer. If you work at McDonalds, you may be working on a computerized cash register, for instance. It is no longer practical or logical to ignore the technology of the PC. It's not like it was in the 70s when you really had to be a geek to have a computer, and in the 80s you really didn't need them unless you worked in the computer industry directly. Ambitious professionals carried laptops with Win 3.x on them in the early 90s, but that was about the only segment of the population that had computers except for people that were studying Computer Science. Nowadays, computers are everywhere and dot com companies are coming out by the dozens. All walks of life are getting online and socioeconomics aren't much of a factor anymore. Lower-class people may end up with used computers in a lot of cases, but they are getting on the Internet more and more one way or another. Wake up and smell the 21st century: There is no reason to be proud about a lack of computer knowledge. Furthermore, there is no reason not to have a computer. They have come down in price to the point where sometimes you can get a nice full system for $500 or less if you're really lucky. Well, at least with rebates it might end up being in that range, but there are many full systems with a printer for under a grand. You are disadvantaged these days if you don't own a PC. If you have kids, they will be disadvantaged in school without a computer, and you are partitioning yourself off from lots of information—lots of free information at that.

The Internet has closed the gap a bit between the wealthy and the poor or middle class. No more can only the privileged have access to just about any kind of information!

Guess what folks? Computers are not going away; they are the wave of the future. The beginning of the 21st century is setting the stage for the future of the electronic age. Used to be you could wait to catch up to technology, but now is the time to get your foot in the door and learn.

Acknowledgements

I want to thank my wife Angie for her patience during all the time that it took me to write this book when I seemingly may have ignored her. I also thank her for helping me at times do some of the more menial tasks required in bringing this book to print.

Primer #1

WHAT TO DO WITH YOUR NEW COMPUTER

You just brought your computer home, and you have a deer-in-the-head-lights-and-yet-proud look on your face as you take it out of the box. You should at least skim the manuals and see if you can look for things with an ! (exclamation point) next to them as they are probably the ones that are most important.

Basically, there are just a few cables that hook the computer together, and it isn't nearly as complicated as it seems at first glance. The reasons why the wiring isn't that difficult is that usually there is a guide that tells you exactly how to hook them up, and some of the cables can really only go one way. For example, if you look at the back of the *monitor* (the TV like component), you will notice that it has a certain type of connector that only one of the cables can fit into. On the *tower unit* (the box that contains all the computer hardware such as the CD-ROM drive) there will usually be only one place to accommodate the other end of that cable. The point is that if you take an intelligent look at everything and forget that it's a computer for a minute, you will probably be able to hook these things up without a problem. There is a speaker system that usually has a little schematic with it. This is easy because it's not an electronics schematic mind you; all you have to do is copy the way the wires are hooked up on the diagram that comes with the speakers.

There is a monitor plug that plugs directly from the back of the monitor into a standard electrical outlet in your home that uses 110v. These are the same outlets where you will usually plug any standard home appliance such as a television or a toaster. You then have a cord that goes from the monitor to the tower unit (computer box) as mentioned previously.

Finally, the *mouse*, the *keyboard*, and the *speakers* plug into the tower unit. Just follow the wiring diagram that should have come with your computer if you are confused here. If you can't find a diagram, call your computer manufacturer, and their technical support department should be able to walk you through plugging everything up. If you purchased your computer from a retail store, call and see if they have an extra diagram that you can pick up.

HOW DO I PLUG THE MODEM INTO THE PHONE LINE?

The better question at this point may be just what the heck is a modem? A *modem* is kind of like a telephone, but it's hard to think of it that way because it doesn't have a hand receiver or a number touch pad. Furthermore, the modem is usually inconspicuously placed inside the computer box, so most people lose sight of the fact that it is even there at all. The modem plugs into a standard telephone jack just like a telephone. It has the ability to dial a phone number over the telephone line, and that is how you can connect to an *Internet service provider* (ISP) such as America Online. Without a modem, you wouldn't be able to get outside of your home, and your computer would be reduced to a word processor and an arcade gaming system. That is what it was like before the late 1980s for the most part. Keep in mind that because your modem is like a telephone, when it dials a phone number to connect to your Internet provider, you will get an expensive phone bill if that phone number is long-distance in relation to you. You will need to check with your phone company to see if a particular number is long-distance if there is any doubt in your mind. Your ISP (Internet service provider) will not be able to answer this question because they will not have access to the information that the phone company has. The ISP would need to be able to tap into the telephone companies database in order to know if a number is long-distance in relation to a particular individual or geographical area.

Yes, to get online you will have to connect your modem into the telephone line.

This will require a standard phone cord. One will usually come with your computer or modem if you purchased your modem separately. Pretty nice of em huh?

In the back of the computer there are usually 2 places to plug a phone cord. One is labeled Line and the other Phone. At least one will have an inscription of a little phone next to it and the other what looks like a smaller picture of the end of a phone wire. You plug one end of the phone cord into where it is labeled Line or it might be called Telco (stands for Telephone Company). The other end of the phone line goes into a phone jack in the wall (where you would ordinarily plug a telephone). The phone plug in back of the computer can be used to plug a regular telephone in so you can talk while in front of the computer; it's really just an extra "convenience" jack that gives you an extra phone plug. If you have a laptop computer, there will usually only be one place to plug the phone cord, so there will be no confusion here.

WHAT IF I HAVE AN EXTERNAL MODEM?

There is such a thing as an *external modem*. These devices are shaped kind of like a VCR, but they are about 1/3 the size of one. They kind of resemble a cable box, but external modems usually have a lot of status lights on the front of them that tell you such things as whether they are currently sending or receiving data across the phone line. They remind me of a cross between a cable box and an equalizer that you would integrate into a home stereo system. I had a Yamaha equalizer once that had about 20 of those status bars that spanned nearly all the way across the front of it. The blue LED status lights pulsated to the tones and the beat of the music. With an external modem, you have to integrate it into your computer setup much like you would integrate an equalizer into a rack stereo system. Externals work on the same principle as an internal modem. You plug a phone cord into one place and run the other end into the wall, and there will be an extra place to plug a phone into the modem, in most cases, to give you an extra phone jack. The main difference between an internal and an external modem, besides the obvious, is the way that you reset them. Sometimes modems need to be reset or else they will refuse to dial out. If the modem has been working fine and all of a sudden you can't connect to your ISP, it is a safe bet that the modem needs to be reset. To reset an internal modem, it is necessary to shut the computer down and start it up again. Restarting the computer won't do it; you actually have to shut down. Just turning the modem off and back on can reset an external modem.

I CAN'T HAVE THE COMPUTER ON I ONLY HAVE ONE PHONE LINE!

A common misconception is that you can't talk on the phone while sitting in front of the computer. Sure you can. You can't sign on to your ISP and talk on the phone at this point in time unless you have 2 separate phone lines (a dedicated phone line for the computer). However, *ADSL* and other high-speed media like a *cable modem* are apt to change that. Your modem doesn't access the telephone line until you click on **Sign On, Connect, Ok, Go, Dial**, or whatever it is to connect to your Internet provider. So you can be in front of the computer on the *Desktop* and talk on the phone. The Desktop is the first screen that appears (or should appear) when your computer first starts up. Anyway, you just follow the instructions to set the things up step by step, and it will be pretty straight-forward. Don't be discouraged if things don't go that smoothly. Sometimes Murphy's Law may come into play here—Anything that can go wrong may do so.

HOW TO START UP AND SHUT DOWN

This is something that could be learned from reading the freaking manual (RTFM). You can damage your computer by shutting it down improperly over and over again. You can also damage or corrupt programs that are open at the time that you shut the computer down improperly. However, sometimes the computer may freeze, and you have no choice but to shut the computer down. You can even just unplug it. Just don't turn it right back on! Wait about 10-15 seconds so that the hard drive has a chance to spin down, and then turn it back on. It'll be all right. The computer runs something called *scandisk* that scans the disk for errors and usually has the ability to self-fix them. It will tell you to "press any key" to run scandisk, so press any key at all on the keyboard and it will run it's cycle and usually start up normally unless you deleted some files that you shouldn't have ;-)

To properly start up your computer, just hit the button on the tower unit usually labeled **POWER**. Sometimes there will even be a power switch on the back. You can check in your computer owner's manual. Look in the Index under start or power, and it will tell you how to start the system. Some of the newer systems—that I would define as no older than one year—have what is called a *soft power button*; it is necessary to hold the button in for 5 seconds with these. If you don't hold the button in for that amount of time, nothing will happen at all when you hit the power button.

In order to shut down your computer properly, you should click on **Start** then choose **Shut Down** and click in the middle of the little circle next to where it says Shut Down then click **Ok**. Most computers nowadays will shut themselves down after that. However, sometimes the computer will show a message "It is now safe to shut down your computer" on a black screen, and then you know that you can hit the switch to shut the unit off. You don't want to just hit the power button to turn off the computer when you are in a program or on the Desktop screen (where all the icons are and the START button). If you have Windows Millennium edition (Windows Me), instead of the little circles where you put the black dot, called *radio dials*, there will be a *drop-down menu* when you go to turn off your computer. A drop-down menu has a little down arrow or what looks like a triangle pointing downwards, and when you click on it, it drops down a menu of choices from which you can click on the one that you want. Windows Me will have the choices Shut down, Restart, or Standby when you go to shut down the computer. If you don't see anything that looks similar to what I have described, then you may have another version of Windows such as Windows 2000. Consult the manual on how to safely shut down your computer if nothing looks similar to what I have described. If you have a soft power button, you will need to hold the button in for several seconds to shut the computer down as well as to start it up.

There is a setting in the *BIOS* that defines how much of a delay there will be with a soft power button. If you want the delay reduced or increased, check with the manufacturer or the computer manual. The BIOS is something that controls a lot of the settings on your computer that are behind the curtain so to speak. It is similar to the *Registry* in that respect, but unlike the Registry, you enter the BIOS when the computer is booting up. It will usually tell you what key to press to get into the BIOS. For example, it will say "press ESC to enter setup" or "press F1 to enter setup." I would not advise entering the BIOS unless you know what you are doing. If you do make changes in there, write down what the settings were originally so that if the computer doesn't boot anymore, you can press the key to enter setup while the computer is starting and change the settings back. As a matter of fact, it is a good idea to write down all of the BIOS settings just in case they ever get altered; that is generally the only time that you need to go into the BIOS.

SHOULD I SHUT DOWN MY COMPUTER OR LEAVE IT ON?

This question is debatable because a lot of computer technicians will probably tell you that you should leave the computer on all the time. I have not found any advantage to leaving the computer on all the time except for the fact that you don't have to wait for it to start up when you are ready to use it. To me it is the same as coming home from work in the evening and letting your car run in the driveway all night until you are ready to leave out in the morning. A good rule of thumb is to turn the computer off if you are going to be away from it for more than a few hours. At least shut it down at night or if you aren't going to be using it for at least 8 to 10 hours. The computer needs to be rebooted anyway once in a while in order to clear the memory and rejuvenate the computer's resources. If the computer's resources run low, it may freeze up the system, you might get an illegal operation error message, it may be sluggish, or you might get a Fatal OE error message. It is surprising how may computer problems can be fixed simply by rebooting the machine.

Primer #2

HOW DO YOU CONNECT?

Have you ever wondered how you connect to your online service? An ingenious device called a modem does this. A modem **mo**dulates and **dem**odulates information hence the name **MO-DEM**. I know your probably saying whoooooooooa! You're getting technical on me! Not really. All this means is that the modem turns the information from your computer into a form that can be sent over a phone line. When you receive information from your ISP, the modem does the opposite: It turns the information from the phone line into a form that the computer can understand. The modem is what enables you to connect to a remote computer. Without the modem, your computer could not reach any ISP or get outside of your home, and it would be a worthless box that would only be good for word processing and computer games. Wait a minute, that sounds like the PC in the early 80s.

The modem is just like a telephone but it does not have a receiver so it is hard to think of it as a phone. There are typically 2 places to plug a phone cord in the back of your computer. One is labeled LINE and the other is labeled PHONE. You will want to take a phone wire and run one end into the jack labeled LINE and attach the other end into a working phone jack in the wall. Just like a telephone, this will allow the modem to dial out over your phone line. The jack on the computer tower unit labeled PHONE is just an optional convenience jack where you could plug a phone if you wanted to. It is not necessary for operation, however. You might want to plug a phone in there if your modem took up your only phone jack in the computer room and you don't want to fork the $100 or so the phone company will charge you to sink another jack in that room.

That way you could talk on the phone while you are in front of the computer. You will not be able to talk on the telephone while your modem is actually connected to your ISP. This would require 2 phone lines. I'm not talking about 2 phone jacks, but you would need to be paying your telephone company for 2 different telephone numbers.

YOU CAN HAVE YOUR COMPUTER ON AND TALK ON YOUR TELEPHONE AT THE SAME TIME WITH JUST ONE PHONE LINE!

That is correct; you can even open up your online services software (sometimes called the Sign on screen or Connect screen) with just one phone line. The modem will not actually access the telephone line until you click **Connect, Sign On, Dial**, or whatever it is to dial-up your online service provider. If another resident in your household is talking on the telephone, you won't be able to sign online unless you have 2 separate phone lines. It would be the equivalent of you picking up the phone and trying to make a call (with just one phone line) while another person in the household is already talking on the telephone. You would barge in on the other person's conversation wouldn't you? However, you will be able to have the computer on and talk on the telephone at the same time. You don't need the modem or the modem doesn't need the phone line until you actually connect to your ISP. Bringing up some sort of Sign-on or Connect screen doesn't mean you're connected either. The modem will not actually be in use until you click on SIGN ON or CONNECT or DIAL, etc. Notice that I reiterated that principle several times because it is a hard concept to grasp at first.

HOW CAN I BE SURE THAT MY ACCESS NUMBER IS A LOCAL CALL FOR ME?

There will be certain numbers that you will select that your modem will dial to connect to your ISP. Usually, on your computer during the registration process you will be asked to enter in your 3-digit telephone area code. A list will come up with all of the numbers that your particular online service has available in your area for you to use to connect with them. The list may include all the numbers listed by city in alphabetical order that the ISP has available. You want to pick some numbers here that look like they are going to be a local call. If you have any doubts, jot the numbers down that you pick at the time and ask your telephone company if these numbers are going to be a local call or a long-distance call for you. Your Internet provider will not be able to tell you this information. Remember, when your modem dials a phone number, it is just like you picked up your phone and dialed that same number. In the same fashion, if you connect to your ISP with a long-distance number, your ISP will not bill you, but you will be billed by the telephone company. Therefore, you will have no recourse with your ISP about the phone bill. How can the ISP credit you for something that they didn't bill you for in the first place? Believe me that there is no stupid question, and technical support doesn't expect computer experts to call them but rather total beginners. They don't mind this at all as this is their job. But if you want to look ignorant, call your ISP and demand a credit for a big phone bill. On the other hand, they may be able to credit you some time on the service to help compensate you for your phone bill. If they do issue credit, it will be completely out of courtesy and not something that they have to do, however. In most cases, your ISP doesn't own the phone numbers that are available. They just rent these numbers from the phone company, and in most cases the ISP has very little or no control over the phone numbers. The bottom line is that it is your responsibility to ensure that you are not dialing a long-distance number.

Furthermore, it is a safe bet that any ISP is going to have a disclaimer that addresses the phone number subject, so you will have no legal ground to stand on. Most people don't realize this because they don't take the time to read the long diatribe that will be presented to you during registration.

WHERE SHOULD I BE WHEN CALLING TECH SUPPORT?

When calling technical support, it is a good idea to be in front of your computer if you are having any kind of technical problem whatsoever. It would not be necessary of course if you had a question about a free trial or your billing or something of that nature. You see if you are disconnecting from your ISP when you don't intend to or something like that, the technician is going to want to know some things about your computer. The computer will have to be on for you to find this information out for them. Technicians are not mind readers (most of the time), and they will usually just tell you to call back when you are in front of your computer if your problem involves anything technical. Also, they won't be able to just give you instructions most of the
time because sometimes they can be quite involved, and if you know enough to follow through with them, you probably won't need to call tech support in the first place. And if you are that much of an expert, then you probably won't be reading this. See Appendix A, *What to do and What to Expect When Calling Tech Support,* for more on this subject.

JUST TELL ME HOW TO FIX MY COMPUTER PROBLEM!

Another thing that most people don't realize is that any given problem can have many possible resolutions. As a matter of fact, there is rarely a computer problem that has just one clear-cut solution. If you are a mechanic or a doctor or you have a profession that requires some kind of troubleshooting, you can probably appreciate this. That squeak under the hood of your car could be anything from a loose fan belt to the engine needing oil or an oil change. Would you call your mechanic and describe the problem or would you drive to the garage and let him see or hear it for himself? If you did call your mechanic about a car problem, chances are he would tell you to bring it in anyway. With a computer it is no different.

Any given problem will typically have different resolutions based on many variables such as how much memory your computer has, what type of modem you have, or what software you have installed on your computer. That is why sometimes when you call tech support, they may not get the problem fixed the first time. This is especially true if you only have one phone line because all they can do sometimes is take an educated guess and hope it works. If they can't test their fix by having you sign online while you are still on the phone, they may not be sure that the fix is going to work.

Something that I want to point out is that not only can you have the computer on and talk on the phone, but most of the time technical support for an ISP will not need you to be able to sign online while you are talking to them. It may be useful for you to be able to sign on while talking to your ISP's tech support but only to test what they have done to fix your problem. Your ISP's software works hand in hand with your computer; they are both intertwined. Therefore, if something isn't working correctly with your ISP, it is more than likely going to require an adjustment in Windows to correct it. On the same token, if the ISP's software doesn't run correctly on your computer, there is a good chance that you have computer problems. It is usually either a problem in Windows or damaged ISP software when something doesn't go right with your ISP. Reinstalling your ISP's software will fix the latter. If the problem doesn't relate to Windows or the ISP's software, then chances are that whatever problem you are experiencing is host-based, meaning that it is something on the ISP's end that they will need to fix and there is nothing that can be done on your individual computer to help the situation.

There may be 50 different things that could cause a certain problem. When troubleshooting, a technician will usually do the most likely fix based on the circumstances (the kind of computer configuration that you have) and the problem that you are having. If that doesn't work, they go to the 2nd most likely fix and so on and so on. It wouldn't make sense to do all 50 fixes at once because there is a good chance that the 1st or 2nd fix will do it. Doing every possible fix all at once not only can be a waste of time, but it can actually break something else in certain situations if it turns out that the last 49 fixes were not necessary. Furthermore, if you do too many things at once, it will not be clear which one actually fixed the problem. Therefore, a technical consultant will typically try two or three different things for a certain problem and send you on your way to test it. You may find yourself calling back again and again which will be frustrating to say the least. Rest assured that a technician does want to fix your problem, and there is nothing a technician wants less than an irate customer. So do yourself a favor and save yourself some time; be in front of the computer with the computer on when you call tech support.

Primer #3

SOFTWARE AND HOW IT WORKS

We are almost ready to start the first chapter, but I thought that I would keep you in suspense through one more primer first. I know—very funny. No really I thought there were a few more things that we should go over before officially getting started with the actual lessons in this book. Before we hit the tutorials, I want to make sure that you can get your computer up and running and even get online.

Even if you have made it online already, let's talk about ISP (Internet service provider) *software* a little bit so you can gain an understanding of how it works. A piece of software is a program that can be installed on your computer. A program is a set of instructions that tell the computer how to act. These days software usually comes on a CD ROM just like a music CD-ROM that you can play on a stereo. Incidentally, you can play an audio CD in your computer's CD-ROM drive provided that the computer has a program that is capable of playing audio tracks. Most of the time a program that can play audio tracks, called CD Player, will come already loaded on your computer. Another thing that is important to point out: You should **not** put a data CD-ROM into your stereo CD player! It will ruin your speakers. A data CD is any CD that does not have audio tracks on it. So while you can put an audio CD into your computer CD-ROM, the process is not interchangeable because you only want to put data CDs in your computer's CD-ROM drive and not in the stereo CD player.

A computer consists of *hardware* and software. Hardware is anything tangible like the keyboard, mouse, or monitor. Software will be on a CD usually, and even though you can touch a CD and therefore call it tangible, it is still considered software because it contains a program (series of instructions) that you can install on your computer.

Sometimes, software will come on a 3 ½" floppy disk, but a floppy disk will only hold a fraction of the information compared to what a CD-ROM will hold. These days the increasing complexity of programs makes them very memory intensive. They require a lot of room to store all of the data, so many programs won't fit on a floppy disk anymore. Programs can also be downloaded from the Internet. See Appendix D, *Downloading Files From the Internet,* for general information on the subject.

HOW TO SIGN ON TO YOUR ISP

When you go to sign onto an ISP, you will need to install some software. Many ISPs software will come preinstalled on your computer. With a new computer these days, either AOL or CompuServe 2000 will probably be preinstalled which means that you don't need a CD to install them. You could just double-click on the AOL or CompuServe icon and follow the onscreen prompts in order to get online. Sometimes these ISPs will be located in a folder called Online Services. Click **Start>Programs>Online Services**. By the way, the symbol (>) will be used from here on out in this book to describe a path to get somewhere on the computer. In this context, the > symbol means then. i.e. Click **Start** then **Programs** then **Online Services.**

RULES OF THE ROAD

Some other consistencies that you will find in this book are as follows: Terms found in the Glossary will be in *italics* and **bold** such as ***Internet.*** Some terms may be found in the Glossary that are not italicized or bolded—that are not even mentioned in this book for that matter. In the effort to put together a comprehensive Glossary, I tried to make it as complete as possible even if there are entries that are not in this book. Every word that is outlined in the book will be found in the Glossary. You may run across a term that you feel should be in the Glossary that isn't. Terms such as these will be defined in the writing itself, and I may have felt that it would be redundant or superfluous in certain situations to mention such terms in the Glossary.

Keyboard commands will be in all caps and bold. i.e., **CTRL+ALT+DELETE**. Steps that you actually click on will be highlighted and capitalized. However, the whole word will not be capitalized but just the first letter. i.e., click **Start>Settings>Control Panel**. Important items will be capitalized for emphasis, but they will not be bolded. These will include some of the same words that you will see in bold throughout this book, but if they are not direct instructions to click on, they will not be bolded. For example, if I said, "When you click on the Start button the Programs menu will ensue," you would notice that the word Start and Programs are capitalized but not bolded. Furthermore, other words that are descriptive, and that I think require a little extra emphasis will be capitalized. For example, you will notice that in a modem description, I will say "You need to plug the phone cord into the Line port in the modem and the other end goes into the phone jack in the wall." There will be some exceptions to these rules, but for the most part they will be consistent. Deviations from these rules usually have a good reason. I will not get into all of these, but one example is if a term that is in the Glossary has already been mentioned, it will not be italicized and bolded if it is mentioned a 2nd time. If you look hard enough, you can probably find inconsistencies that are simply a mistake on my part. I apologize in advance if you run across one of these. It is extremely difficult to adhere to all of these rules throughout a book of this size, and to be honest I am far from perfect. Also, there were some ambiguous situations that I ran across with these rules where I probably could have done things more than one way and still have been correct—or incorrect.

WHAT ISP SHOULD I CHOOSE?

I would highly recommend going with AOL or CompuServe 2000 at least for your first online experience. Both ISPs offer a 30 day/100 hr. free trial. That's 30 days or 100 hrs. whichever comes first. The promotion may extend to 30 days/500 hrs. whichever comes first during certain promotional periods. For the most part, the free trial usually ends up being 30 days free because people will rarely exceed the hourly limitation within that time period. You really have nothing to lose by trying these free trials, and you might find that you really like one of these services and stay with them. The reason why I would recommend AOL or CompuServe 2000 (especially if you have never been online) is that these are by far the easiest ISPs to operate. And if you are a beginner, you will probably be very frustrated with a *plain-vanilla ISP*. If you have a hard time with AOL, which is entirely possible as a beginner, you will never be able to navigate a standard ISP. Once you become 'Net-savvy, you may decide that you want to try a standard ISP. There's certainly nothing wrong with trying a variety of ISPs and then settling on the one that you like best. Almost any ISP offers some sort of a free trial. So be adventurous and explore if you want to. There is no best and worst ISP per se, but it is really a matter of opinion. One man's trash is another man's treasure or that's why Baskin Robbins has 31 flavors because everybody has different tastes.

For the purposes of this primer, I will assume that you are going to register for AOL or CompuServe 2000 although they all work in a similar manner as far as registration is concerned. If the ISP software didn't come preinstalled on the computer, you may have received a CD for AOL or CompuServe with all the other CDs that should have come with your computer. If you have a CD for an ISP, just put it into your CD-ROM drive. If you are confused as to where your CD-ROM drive is, refer to your computer manual. It is usually on the front of your tower unit, and it has a slide-out drawer. Start pressing buttons on the front if you have to, and when the drawer slides out, you will know that you have found it. You won't hurt anything. The worst that can happen is that you hit the power button and turn the computer off, and that is still no crime. Just wait at least 10 seconds and turn it back on. It will be all right.

When you put a CD-ROM into the drive and close the door, the installation program should start to run automatically, and from there it is pretty intuitive to set up. A CD-ROM will typically have one side with writing on it and another side that is shiny. The writing should be facing up when it is inserted into the CD-ROM drive. These programs have become so easy to install that you really don't need any computer knowledge at all to install them, rather just a little common sense. All you have to do with these programs is click **Next** or **Yes** or whatever it is to continue with the operation all the way through the installation. So if you are confronted with a choice of OK or Cancel, click **OK**. If the choice is Next or Exit, click **Next**. Furthermore, these programs usually will default to the "New User" settings. Default settings on a computer mean how the settings come preset from the factory. In other words, the default settings are how things will automatically be set if you don't change them. So when I say that it defaults to the New User settings, it means that if you come to a screen that has several choices, it will automatically be set on the one that you want in order to create a new account with the ISP. Thus, you would not need to change anything but merely click **Next, OK, Continue,** or whatever the choice is to proceed.

Don't get confused with the ***Internet Connection Wizard*** if you are trying to sign up for a certain ISP. The Internet Wizard is something that will run automatically sometimes when you first turn on your computer. Or you can launch the Connection Wizard by clicking on the icon that says

Internet Explorer on your Windows Desktop. This wizard is merely the setup for the Microsoft Internet Explorer browser. Internet Explorer and other browsers are discussed more thoroughly in *Compquest Volume 2* in the Internet chapters such as Chapter 20, *The Internet Part II*. For right now all you need to know is that this wizard just defines how the Web browser is configured. The configuration will vary depending on what ISP you have. Also, the Connection Wizard will lead a new computer user into signing up for MSN (The Microsoft Network), which is another ISP that offers a free trial that you may want to try.

If you find yourself in the middle of the Connection Wizard setup, you are not signing up for your ISP necessarily. Also, it is difficult to get out of the Connection Wizard sometimes. If you find yourself stuck in here, press **CTRL+ALT+DELETE (DEL)** simultaneously once on your keyboard and it should bring up a *Close Program window*. This window will show you every program that is currently running in the background on your computer. The first listing at this point should be Internet Connection Wizard. Just make sure that listing is highlighted, or click on it to highlight it, and click on **End Task** at the bottom left. This should get you out of the program. If not, repeat the procedure again, and if any kind of message pops up, click **End Task** on it. This is a good ploy to get out of a stuck computer when you just can't seem to close a program. Keep in mind that if you press **CTRL+ALT+DELETE** twice rapidly, it will restart your computer (called a warm boot). If your computer is totally frozen, even a *warm boot* may not restart the computer. In this kind of situation, all you can really do is manually shut the computer off or unplug it if it still won't turn off. This normally won't hurt the computer, but just make sure you wait about 10-15 seconds before turning the computer back on. This is not the proper way to shut a system down, and it should not be shut off this way as a rule. But if the computer is completely frozen, you may not have any choice but to just shut the machine off.

ISP REGISTRATION

The registration for an ISP like AOL is all done online (on your computer). There normally isn't a need to call tech support to sign up unless you run into a snag and need some technical help or the program reaches a point that tells you to call customer service to verify your billing information or something of that nature. After the program is installed on your computer, it will detect what kind of modem you have. Then it will need the telephone line to dial out where it will connect to the registration server of your ISP. The modem hookup we already covered in the previous primers. The registration screen will ask for such info as your name, address, phone number, and billing or payment information. When you are entering this information, you are connected to a remote server. A *server* is just a computer that is dedicated to a specific purpose. In this case the purpose would be handling new registrations. When you enter in your billing info, it is very secure, and there is no need for you to worry about your info getting into the wrong hands (at least with the large major ISPs; I can't speak for every ISP out there) because the server is secure. It is at least as safe (probably safer) to put your credit card info here then if you whip out your credit card at a gas station or a place where someone could see your credit card number. If you are still leery about typing your info in here, some ISPs such as AOL offer over-the-phone registration.

You may ask why do I need to put in credit card info anyway if this is a free trial? Valid question and there is a simple answer. First of all it serves as some sort of verification that the new customer is at least 18 years of age which is a legal requirement. I mean a child could take their parents credit card and sign up, but it at least weeds out some cases where a minor will try and register. Also, it is up to parents to secure their credit cards, so if the kids get it, it is the parent's responsibility. Secondly, by asking for your billing information up front, it allows the ISP to have your info already on record, so at the end of the trial period there is no action required on your part to stay signed on. Since the ISP still has your payment info, your free trial account will just be converted to a paid account at the end of your trial time. Therefore, it saves you from having to call and tell them you want to remain a customer if you want to keep the account. If you want to keep it, just continue using your Internet provider like you did during the trial period.

WHAT'S THE FREE TRIAL OFFER?

One thing you want to be aware of is what type of account you will have at the end of your trial period. At the time I am writing this, in October 2000, AOL will automatically put you on the $21.95 unlimited plan. CompuServe 2000 will default to the $9.95/20 hrs plan. Realize that this only gives you 20 hrs of use per month for your monthly membership fee of $9.95. Each additional hour is $2.95. So if you want CompuServe's unlimited plan for $19.95, you need to either call and tell them that you want to switch to unlimited pricing within your trial period or make the change yourself online. You can make changes like this at Keyword billing on AOL or CompuServe 2000.

Let me repeat that CompuServe's free trial deal right now defaults to the limited plan. Be aware of this because it can really catch you off guard. If you say or do nothing, about 30 days after you sign up with CompuServe 2000 you will be billed $9.95 for 20 hours. So the 2nd month if you are online 100 hrs, the first 20 hrs are covered in your $9.95 membership fee, and you will owe for the other 80 hrs—that would be 80 x $2.95 in addition to the $9.95 monthly membership fee. In that example, your monthly bill would be $245.95 (80 x $2.95= $236+$9.95=$245.95). If you keep the service past the trial period and you switch to the unlimited service, you will be billed $19.95 after about 30 days, and that will give you unlimited service the next month. AOL defaults to the unlimited access plan, which means that if you say or do nothing during your trial period, after approximately 30 days you will be billed $21.95 which pays for the upcoming month. About 30 days after that you will be billed another $21.95 and so on, so you really end up paying for the month in advance because you get the 30-day free trial. AOL does give you unlimited access for your $21.95; there are no hourly charges on their unlimited plan. Of course, there are no hourly charges on CompuServe's unlimited plan either. Both of these services do not have an annual contract unless you knowingly subscribe to one to gain a discount or a rebate. That means that you can pay month to month and cancel at any time. However, if you have already been billed for the current month, you may not be able to recoup the membership fee for that month even if you didn't use your entire 30 days worth. If you have any doubts about this, check with your ISP's billing department to get some clarification.

Another thing to point out is if the free trial period is 30 days or 100 hrs, you will be billed for all hours that you use over 100 hrs in that first 30 days. There are special promotions that you will see sometimes on a CD such as one that AOL or CompuServe might send in the mail. These might offer 250 hours or 500 hours or 30 days whichever comes first instead of just 100 hours. Just make sure that you understand the trial period so you don't end up with a surprise bill at the end of the month. One more thing is that you normally can't change your pricing plan in the middle of the month. Let's look at this scenario: You try the free trial of CompuServe 2000, which is 30 days or 100 hrs whichever happens first. You use 105 hours in your free trial, so you will owe for the 5-hour overage. That would come to 5 x $2.95 or about 15 bucks. You don't opt for unlimited use, so after 30 days you get charged $9.95, giving you 20 free hours in the up and coming month. (Remember with AOL it defaults to unlimited use, so you would be billed $21.95 after your trial, and you would be on the unlimited plan that would allow for unlimited use the next month). You reach your 20 hrs after the 1st week, and you realize that maybe you should have opted for the unlimited plan because you still have

3 weeks of the month to go at $2.95 per hour. You call the billing dept. and tell them that you want the unlimited plan. They tell you that it will take effect on your next billing date which means that you will have 3 weeks that you either will not be able to go online or pay $2.95/hr. Because of the way the whole billing system works, there's not much that they can do to switch you in the middle of a billing cycle. However, in certain circumstances, they may be able to give you some free time to compensate you for it at least a little bit but don't count on it.

Once you have signed onto your ISP you may be offered the chance to download an upgrade. If you do download an upgrade to a whole different version, say AOL 5.0 to AOL 6.0, you will have the setup file on your computer. This setup file is just like having a CD, but when you download a program like that, it is on your computer's big disk (called a hard disk) rather than on a compact disk. This means that you could reinstall the program without having a CD. Incidentally, something I forgot to mention is that after you do install the program you can take the CD out of the CD-ROM drive and put it away somewhere. It is a good idea not to throw this away because you never know when you might need it later. After you run the installation program from the CD, it is also on your hard drive. It basically copies the whole thing from the CD to your hard drive, so you won't need that CD anymore unless it becomes necessary to reinstall your program later on. All you do to sign onto your ISP is click on the icon on your main Windows screen. That will bring up the Sign-On screen, and normally you just need to type in your password and click on **Sign On** or **Connect**.

If you accidentally wipe your ISP software off of your computer and need to reinstall, it may be possible to use a file that you have downloaded. However, if you deleted your software or you had to run the restore disk for your computer, that setup file is not going to be on the computer anymore anyway. You will need a CD to reinstall your ISP software on the computer. AOL and CompuServe send promotional CDs out in the mail all the time. If you didn't get one originally, and you get one in the mail, it would be a good idea to stash the CD somewhere just in case. AOL and CompuServe 2000 typically distribute their CDs at certain outlets so that they are easily accessible for their members or potential members. Some of these places at the present time include Circuit City, Barnes & Noble bookstores, Radio Shack, Blockbuster Video, Office Depot, CompUSA, and Wal-Mart. So if you find yourself in need of a CD, you may want to call some of these places and see if they have a CD you can pick up. If they do have one, it will be free, and you can just run in there and get it. Your ISP will send you a CD at no cost even if you aren't a member yet, but it will usually take 7-10 working days for it to get to you. They usually don't have the facilities to overnight you a CD even if you are willing to pay for it.

I HAVE TO CHANGE COMPUTERS, IS MY ACCOUNT CANCELLED?

You will have an account with your ISP whether you have your ISP software installed on your computer or not. You will still continue to get billed and receive your e-mail whether you have your ISP software installed on your computer or for that matter whether you even have a computer. You see the e-mail is stored on your ISPs computers, called mail servers, and the mail will sit and wait for you until the next time that you sign on. Most ISPs will erase your mail after about 30 days so that their mail servers won't get overloaded. The point that I am making is that your Internet service remains on their computers, and all you have to do is draw a connection between you and your ISP if you erase the original software, get a new computer, get a 2nd computer or somehow lose connection with them. Like I was explaining earlier, when you are signing on as a new member, you leave everything set on the defaults that are usually going to be for a new registration. When you already have an account set up, and you need to reinstall your ISP to get reconnected with them, you just need to change the default settings to the choice you will see that says something like "I want to add my existing account to the computer" or "I already have an account I'd like to use" or something similar.

In the case of America Online, you would choose "I already have an AOL account I'd like to use." When you choose this option, where it ordinarily would say "Type your registration number in here," it will change to "Type in your screen name," and where it asks for your password you would type in the password that you already picked out to go with your screen name. You would not need to input your billing info again because you did that when you first registered. All you would need to do is type in your screen name and password and click **Next** or **Sign on**. The system will recognize that you have an active account, and you will be back online. The same procedure can be used to install your ISP account on another computer. Your ISP doesn't care if you install your same account on 1000 computers; you would still only be charged for one account. However, while some ISPs like AOL allow for multiple screen names so everyone in the family can have their own e-mail address (The screen name is the same as the e-mail address or more accurately, if the screen name is johnsmith123, the e-mail address would be johnsmith123@aol.com), and you can install your account on multiple computers, only one person or screen name can be signed on at any given time. Simultaneous logons would require 2 separate accounts.

SHOULD I NOTIFY MY ISP IF I GET A DEDICATED PHONE LINE?

One post statement before we get started: Your ISP doesn't care what phone line you plug your modem into. A lot of people are under the impression that they need to notify their ISP when they get a second phone line. All you really need to do is unplug the phone wire from the first phone line and plug it into the second phone line and sign on. The one issue that may arise here is when you have call waiting on the first phone line and not on the second which is the norm. You may have your ISP software configured to dial a code such as *70 to disable call waiting. Disabling call waiting will keep the call waiting beep from making the modem disconnect. In English, this means that it would prevent you from getting bumped offline with an incoming call. If your ISP software is still dialing *70 on a line (like your 2nd phone line) that doesn't have call waiting, you will not get through; it will usually give you an audible operator message or it will say that the number is busy every time. You would need to go into the settings of your ISP to enable call waiting in a case such as that.

If you think about it, it would not be practical to try and keep up with what phone line people are using to dial in with. If this were the case, everyone that hops from hotel room to hotel room would have to call into tech support before signing on. Needless to say this would be very inconvenient to the customer. Now, if you got a new primary phone number, you might want to tell your ISP eventually just to update your billing information.

I got fairly long-winded on this one, but without further adieu let's get on to Chapter 1 *Beginner Computer Tips*.

Chapter #1

Beginner Computer Tips:

I AM JUST NOT A TECHNICAL PERSON

Please don't be offended if you are beyond the skill level addressed in this book. The following chapters were specifically designed for a person that has never worked on a computer and just needs to know some basics. An important element is your willingness to learn because if you don't want to learn, you won't make much progress. It is easy to live a self-fulfilling prophecy by taking the attitude "I'm not a technical person" or "I don't know anything about computers." I worked for a major ISP, and I have taken many technical support phone calls. One of the things that made me cringe was when people said right off the bat "I am just not a technical person." I can relate to what it's like to be a beginner because I have been there myself believe me. I also understand and appreciate people that realize that they don't know much about computers as long as they have an open mind. This class of people will usually follow directions to a tee and won't cynically question every little move.

Let's face it folks. On today's PCs, and with most commercial software, you don't have to be a computer genius to take care of most of your computer needs. All you need is a little common sense and a lot of patience. It's not like it once was when you had to know at least one programming language to get by on your computer. Back then you would have needed to know command lines, parameters, and switches for every little operation. In those days, DOS (Disk Operating System) was prevalent amongst PCs. We have come a long way since then; with most software there is an installation wizard that guides you through the whole thing. If you come to a fork in the road and the choices are lets say Next or Cancel, what are you going to click on? If you want to proceed with the installation of whatever it is, you would choose **Next** of course. This doesn't take any technical ability at all. This only requires the ability to read and a little common sense. With that said let's get on to the fun stuff.

What's coming next are some rudimentary instructions and information. What prompted me to write this guide, and to include the particular subject matter, is that it contains information that I would have wanted to know the first time I took a computer out of the box. I felt that there is such an abundance of information made for the average computer expert, but few books or guides that I have seen have included a set of instructions that are easy to digest and in simple English. Most computer books have some implied knowledge, and I wanted to write something that worked from the ground up. I intended to write this book from a different perspective than others that are equally simplistic. Some of the later lessons in this book get a little technical, but they have the assumed knowledge of the preceding chapters.

FIRST THINGS FIRST

You just got your computer out of the box, and you read those complex instructions that explained how to hook up all the wiring and so forth. After an hour or two (or maybe longer) of toiling over those instructions, and perhaps a call to tech support, you managed to boot the machine into Windows. Now What? Well you probably want to get online, but you need to crawl before you can walk. You need to know some key essentials or your online experience will be frustrating at best. Also, you will no doubt need to call your technical support or your ISP being a beginner. It is really a good idea to learn how to click a mouse or where your START button is before you make that call. Most of the time your technical support will be free with whatever online service you choose. Most of the time they will expect to talk to computer novices and that's fine. I mean if you

knew that much, you probably wouldn't be calling for tech support. However, to call when you haven't read the first word in the instruction manual or had someone show you the very basic things about
your computer is just a frustrating experience for both you and the technical support representative on the other end of the phone. They also realize that there are exceptions. Someone may not have any family members, like a 15 year-old genius that can practically write the next version of Windows, that can show them the basics.

Chapter #2

Computer Components:

The thing that you type on that resembles a typewriter is called a *keyboard*. The first keyboard command that you need to know is **CTRL+ALT+DELETE**. Keyboard commands are a series of 2 or 3 keys that can be pressed simultaneously to perform a certain function. An example of a 2- key command is **CTRL+ESC** that will bring up the Start menu. I will explain this further in the next section, and look at Appendix B, *Shortcut Keys for Windows*, in the back of this book for a list of keyboard commands. The little thing that you slide around on your computer table to move the arrow on your screen is called a *mouse*. The thing that resembles a television set is called a *monitor*, and the box that houses the CD-ROM drive, the floppy drive, and really every other piece of hardware on your computer is called a *tower unit*.

A floppy disk drive is illustrated in **fig. 1** with 2—3 ½" floppy disks in front of it. A tower is shown in **fig. 2** partially disassembled. Notice the motherboard, the big circuit board, at the bottom. If you look closely to the left, you can see all of the cards, such as the sound card, that are plugged into the motherboard.

Fig. 1 Floppy disk drive shown with two 3 ½" floppy disk in front of it.

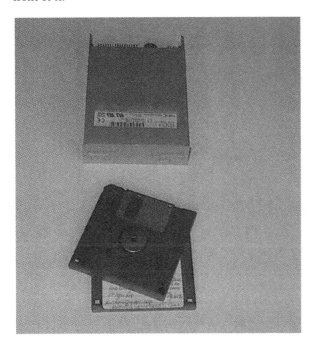

REMEMBER THE MEMORY

Lets talk a little about some of the less obvious parts of your PC and just how they interact. You will hear many terms about a computer that refer to memory, and in case you didn't notice they can be quite confusing. The processor speed isn't really memory, but I grouped it into the memory category because the computer's speed is proportionate to the processor speed just like the memory. More clearly, processor speed is just one of the factors, like memory, that determine the ultimate speed of a computer.

Fig. 2   Tower unit with side
panel removed to show internal
components. Notice the thick
gray ribbon cable and the hard
drive on the bracket in the upper-
left.

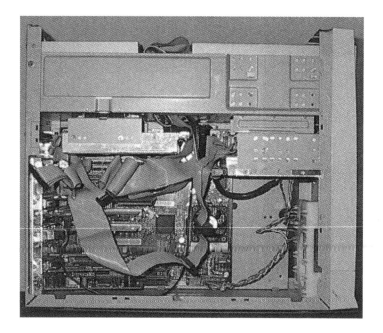

The processor, or *central processing unit* (CPU), is the brain of the computer. Just like the human brain controls the movements of the human
body, the processor controls all of the movements of the hardware. The
term movement is used loosely because there actually are no moving parts
inside the computer to speak of except for the little cooling fan that cools
the CPU. Unlike an automobile, a computer is completely electronic, so
the only movement in a computer is the electrons moving through the
wiring and circuit boards. The speed of the processor will directly relate to
just how fast those electrons can move. The speed of a CPU is expressed in

Megahertz (Mz), and nowadays you might see a 400Mz, a 450Mz, or up to about a 800Mz processor. Just a couple of years ago, a state-of-the-art computer had a 100Mz or 133Mz CPU. Intel processors increased incrementally to 200Mz, 233Mz, 266Mz, 300Mz, 333Mz, and 366Mz respectively. There are state-of-the-art processors already available to the end-user that are 1000Mz {1Gigahertz (Gz)}. It is possible that by the time this book is printed, 1Gz will be just an average machine. As a matter of fact, at the rate that I am going, 1Gz will probably be considered slow by the time this book goes to print.

DON'T FORGET THE RAM EITHER

Another type of memory is RAM memory that basically dictates how many operations a computer can perform at one time and how fast they can be done. The other type of memory is hard drive space. Now think about this analogy: You have a desk. The desktop is the RAM and the drawers, where you can put things for more or less permanent storage, are the hard drive space. If you don't have enough RAM, it would be like if the top of your desk was only 1 foot wide by 1 foot long.

You would be very limited as to how many things you could plop on your desk in that case wouldn't you? If the drawers were full, you would either need to get more drawers, a larger desk, or clean out some of the old junk that is in the drawers to clear out some room for new stuff. The same goes for a hard drive except if your hard drive gets too full, the computer will not run smoothly. It may be very slow, and if it gets too full, the computer may not even start up. This can lead to a computer crash. If your computer crashed, you would probably lose all of the information that you had stored on your computer. In the case of a full hard drive, you would either need to upgrade to a larger hard drive, add a 2nd hard drive, or delete some files on the current hard drive in order to install any new programs on the computer.

Ways to free up drive space:

TIP Some ways to clear some drive space in a pinch are to open up your control panel then Add/Remove Programs. If you see any programs that you don't use or that you have on CD, click once on the program and click the Add/Remove button. The uninstall wizard will walk you through removing the program. If you have the program on a CD, you can always reinstall it when you upgrade your hard drive or have more drive space. If you aren't sure that you can delete a program, skip it and go on to the next one. If you are really low on space, remove every listing out of the Add/Remove list that you can. Generally speaking, all programs can be safely removed from Add/Remove programs. Keep in mind that the program may still be listed even after removal. That is just a listing in Add/Remove Programs, and it does not mean that the program is still on the computer.

Another thing that you can do to clear up drive space is to search for .tmp, .chk, and ~*.* and delete all of them. Click Start>Find>Files or Folders. Start>Search>For Files or Folders if you have Windows Me. On the line where you can type something to search for, type *.tmp, *.chk, ~*.* (separate each file by a comma and a space, and the wavy line is called a tilde; it is usually located in the upper left corner of your keyboard). Make sure that where it says Look In: it is set to the C Drive and click Find Now or Search Now. When it comes up with the findings, click Edit at the top and click Select All. Then click File at the top and click Delete. Say Yes to send all of the files to the recycle bin. All you have to do after that is close the Find Files window and empty the recycle bin. Right-click on recycle bin and left click on Empty Recycle Bin. These files that you are deleting are files that Windows writes to itself from time to time and they are no longer needed after you shut down and restart the computer. In other words, when you close a program, Windows may write some temporary files (.tmp) to itself. When you shut down, they are not needed again. As long as the computer boots the next time, everything will be Ok if you delete these files.

A hard drive is a rectangular shaped object that will be inside the tower unit so you cannot see it. It is usually about 6 inches long by 4 inches wide and about an inch thick. RAM on the other hand is a chip that will be perhaps 4 or 5 inches long and an inch wide. It has the thickness of slightly more than a credit card, and RAM plugs into a slot inside your tower unit. A hard drive will come in memory increments of Gigabytes (GB) these days. Not all that long ago, these drives were expressed in Megabytes (MB). An average size hard drive these days will be around 6 Gigabytes. Actually, the average is already somewhere between 12 and 18 Gigabytes, and a large drive is still considered 20-40 GB. A *kilobyte* (KB) is 1000 bytes, a *Megabyte* (MB) is one million bytes, and a *Gigabyte* (GB) is one billion bytes. Thus, 1000 Megabytes equals 1 Gigabyte.

HOW MUCH MEMORY DO I NEED?

RAM is usually expressed in increments of 8 and in Megabytes (MB). Several years ago, a new computer typically came with 8 MB of RAM. About 2 years ago the new computer standard was 16MB. The standard became 32MB, still the de facto standard although a lot of new systems will come with 64MB of RAM. A power user might have 128MB or even 256MB of RAM, and it won't be too much longer before 512MB of RAM or even 1GB of RAM will be loaded on many PCs. With all of the complex software nowadays, it is very difficult to function with less than 32MB of RAM. If you were buying a new PC now in the fall of 2000, I would highly recommend that you not settle for less than 128MB of RAM memory. With that amount of RAM, you will not have to worry about upgrading your system for a while. On the other hand, I wouldn't really go to the expense of more than 256MB of RAM unless you intend to use your computer mainly for games or high-end graphics work like Computer Aided Design (CAD). Random Access Memory or RAM memory, like most other computer parts, gets cheaper as time goes on. Go as far as 256MB RAM if the extra expense is no big deal to you, and just make sure the computer can be upgraded so that you can add more RAM a year or two down the road when it might be dirt-cheap. You reach a point of diminishing returns with RAM, and it is beneficial to have 128MB at this point in time (fall 2000). However, 64MB will get you by, and over 256MB of RAM is really a waste of money unless you play games or do sophisticated graphics work like I mentioned before. The reason why a huge amount of RAM isn't necessarily better right now is that operating systems haven't even reached the point yet where they can take full advantage of more than about 256MB or RAM. It is analogous to a speedometer on an airplane that goes up to 900,000 mph (miles per hour). On the other hand, if you get 512MB of RAM, you certainly won't have to worry about upgrading for a while but it will put a little dent in your pocketbook.

BASIC KEYBOARD COMMANDS

There are different key combinations that you can press on your keyboard that cause the computer to do specific actions. Like I mentioned, these are called keyboard commands. Early on I wanted to mention the **CTRL+ALT+DELETE** key combination. The CTRL key is located in the lower left corner of your keyboard, and the ALT key is just to the right of it. On modern keyboards there is a Windows key in the middle of the 2 keys. The Windows key can perform some neat functions in combination with other keys, also shown in Appendix B *Shortcut Keys for Windows*. The Delete key will just say DEL on some keyboards and on others it will be spelled out DELETE. There are 6 keys that are grouped together that are next to the number pad (the number pad resembles a calculator) on the far right side of the keyboard. These 6 keys include Insert, Home, Page Up, Delete, End, and Page Down. If you press the **CTRL+ALT+DELETE** keys at the same time, it is supposed to bring up a Close Program window on your computer screen. This window lists all of the programs that are currently running in the background.

SAVE YOUR WORK!

If you get stuck in a program and your computer seems to be locked up, you can try to get out of it by pressing the **CTRL+ALT+DELETE** key combination. Click on the program that you are in currently. You will see it listed probably at the top of the entire list of programs, and it may already be highlighted but if it isn't, just click on it once to highlight it and click on **End Task** at the bottom of the Close Program window. If you are still stuck in the program, repeat the procedure because sometimes it takes two or even several times of doing this too finally end task on a program. If a message pops up on your screen, click on **End Task** on the message and it will go away and close the program that you were stuck in. If you press the CTRL+ALT+DELETE keys twice, it will restart your computer (this is called a warm boot).

If you press the CTRL+ALT+DELETE keys and it doesn't do anything (make sure you held them all down at the same time then let up on all of them), then you are really frozen, and usually the only way out of it is to simply turn the entire computer off. If it won't go off, unplug it. Either way, give it at least 15 seconds to cool down and turn it back on. It may run something called a scandisk while starting up which is normal, and then it should start up okay. It is really not that unusual for a computer to freeze once in a while, but if it happens chronically, you should call your computer manufacturer (if you have a Compaq computer, you should call Compaq. If you have a Gateway, call Gateway, for example) because you may have some configuration problems. Also, be sure to save your work frequently. Some programs have built-in backup features that will save your work every so often, or they will ask you if you want to save your work at certain time intervals. To manually save your work, all you need to do is click on **File** in the upper-left corner in any Windows program and then click on **Save**. If the computer freezes and you End Task or have to shut down, you will probably lose all of the work that you did since the last save so don't say that I didn't warn you.

Chapter #3

The art of Double-clicking

GETTING TO KNOW YOUR MOUSE

Using your mouse is one of the first things that you need to learn when using your computer. Some things require a single-click and some things require a double-click. There is really no easy way to tell somebody which is which. It is the kind of thing that will take a little time; you will learn instinctively when and how to click the mouse. Basically, if you single-click on something and it doesn't open it, or it just turns it blue (or a different color), then try to double-click on it.

You will know the next time that the operation requires a double-click. When you double-click your mouse, it is necessary to click twice in rapid succession or the computer will interpret it as 2 single clicks.

How to adjust mouse click speed

TIP If you never seem to be able to double-click fast enough, or if you are too fast for the computer, you can make the mouse react faster or slower to suit your needs. Open up the control panel and double-click the Mouse icon. On the screen that comes up (Buttons tab), slide the slide bar to the left or right under the Double-click speed section. Double-click the jack-in-the-box to the right, and if he pops out of the box, double-click it again and make him go back in the box. If you aren't able to click fast enough to do this, slide the slide-bar to the left to make the mouse slower. If you think you can handle it a little faster, slide the slide-bar to the right. After you make any adjustment, don't forget to click Apply then OK at the bottom.

If you have a hard time getting the rhythm down with the double-click, you can use your right mouse button. Right-click once on something and it will produce a *drop-down menu*. Left-click **Open** on that menu and as a whole this will serve as a double left-click. You won't use the right-mouse button much until you become proficient on the computer, but I am simply pointing out that it is there and it is an option in a lot of cases. You can experiment by right-clicking on something to see what choices are on the drop-down menu. There are many situations on a computer that provide at least 2 ways to perform a certain function. One example is that you can get to the control panel by clicking **Start>Settings>Control Panel**. If you have trouble with the cascading menu (the menu that slides to the right when you click on Settings), you can get to the Control Panel by double-clicking on **My Computer** then double-clicking **Control Panel**. If you cannot double-click, you can right-click on **My Computer** and left-click on **Open**. Next, right-click on **Control Panel** and left-click **Open**.

If you just can't get the rhythm of the double-click down, you can configure your mouse to make a single-click work as a double-click and simply hovering your mouse over something will serve as a single-click. Open My Computer and click **View>Folder Options** in Windows 98 or **Tools>Folder Options** in Windows Me. Under the *Click items as follows* heading at the bottom, put a dot in the circle next to Single-click to open an item (point to select) and then click **Apply** at the bottom of the Window then **Ok**.

PRACTICE MAKES PERFECT

There are some ways to practice mouse movements with programs that you already have on your computer. The game Solitaire can teach you how to click and double-click as well as how to drag and drop files. To get there from your Windows Desktop (The screen that comes up when you first turn your computer on with the Start button, the Recycle Bin, My Computer, and so forth), click on the **Start** button then choose **Programs** on the Start Menu. You will see a cascading menu to your right. Click on **Accessories** and then click on **Games**. On the menu that slides out to the right from there, click on **Solitaire**. It is pretty self-explanatory from there provided that you have ever played solitaire. If you aren't familiar with the game, click on **Help** at the top then **Help Topics** and choose **Playing Solitaire**. When you drag the cards from the deck to the solitaire piles, this is called dragging and dropping files in computer lingo.

If you cannot locate the games, you can call your computer manufacturer's technical support and they can walk you through installing the games. They may just be located somewhere else other than Accessories, or they may have never been installed in the first place. If you want to try it yourself, you can add all of the game files in Windows by using the Add/Remove programs feature.

Here's how to add the games in Windows 95/98/Me:

Fig. 3   Windows setup screen seen by going into the
Control Panel then Add/Remove Programs.

Click on **Start** then **Settings** and choose **Control Panel**. Double-click on **Add/Remove programs** in the upper-left hand corner of the control panel. Click on **Windows Setup** at the top. Windows may pause at this point and say "Please wait while setup searches for installed components...." This is normal and just wait a few seconds and it will come to another screen with about a dozen or so listings. Click on the **Games** listing and click on **Details**. Put a check mark in every check box on that screen and click **Ok**. Click **Apply** then **Ok** on the next screen. At that point you will need to insert your Windows CD-ROM in the drive and click **Ok**. Your computer will extract the needed files from there, and you can go back and find the games in the Accessories menu as described before. See **fig. 3** and **fig. 4** for illustrations of the Add Programs windows.

Fig. 4   Click Windows Setup at the top of the Add/Remove window.
Click Games then Details at the bottom right.

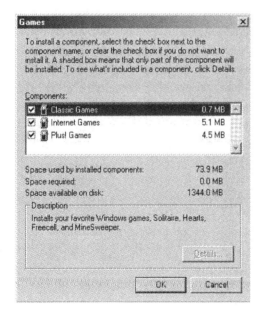

Chapter #4

A Quick Tour of Windows

MORE THAN ONE WAY TO SKIN A CAT

Now that you know about the main hardware components on the computer and how to use the mouse, lets take a look around your computer. I will be throwing a little bit of the lingo out there, but the terms used will be the basics that you need to know. Knowing these terms will help if you need to explain a problem to tech support also. The main screen that comes up when you first turn on your computer is called the *Windows Desktop*. From the Desktop, you can get to anything that you want on the computer. Just like roadways, there is usually more than one way to get to your destination. One is not necessarily better than the other. Sometimes, one way might be quicker but more difficult than the other way to reach your destination. For example, to get to the Control Panel, you can click on **Start>Settings>Control Panel**. That way would be said to be on the Start Menu. That makes sense huh? You see you clicked on Start to get there. Another way to do the same thing is to click on **Start>Run** and type **control** on the line where it says **Open:** then click **Ok.**

CONTROL YOUR CONTROL PANEL

The control panel is where you can adjust virtually any kind of setting that you can make on a computer. You really don't want to play in here too much until you are pretty familiar with your system. Although, you have to remember that you are not going to blow up your computer unless you stuff a stick of dynamite under the tower unit (you might be tempted to do this at first). The worst thing that can really happen is that you will need to reinstall Windows. This is not usually difficult believe it or not, and if you have a new computer, your computer manufacturer's tech support can usually walk you through it. My point is that you can't be scared to try things on your computer. This is how you will learn, and if you end up reinstalling Windows once or twice, so what. The hardest thing about reinstalling Windows is backing up any files that you may have put on your computer. If you run what a lot of computer manufacturers call a restore disk, it will restore your computer to the way it was when you first purchased the computer—assuming that you bought your computer new. Restoring the computer will wipe any files or programs off of the hard drive that you may have installed since you acquired the computer. If you have a new computer, chances are you haven't installed that many programs or have any personal files anyway, so it wouldn't really matter in that case.

MY COMPUTER IS YOUR COMPUTER

If you open up the My Computer icon, you will see all of the drives listed that your computer has, as well as that Control Panel icon I was talking about, and a Printer icon that will just show what printer you have installed on your computer, if any. You will notice an icon in the illustrated My Computer in **fig. 5** called *Dial-up Networking*. This allows someone to make a direct dial-up connection to another computer. Dial-up Networking (DUN) will usually only be used if a user dials into their office network from a laptop computer at home or another remote location. The Scheduled Tasks icon is where you can configure your computer to run computer maintenance tasks, such as *Scandisk* and *Disk Defragmenter*, at time intervals that you specify. If you have a CD-ROM in the drive, Windows has a neat little feature that will show you the name of the CD and then the drive letter of the CD-ROM drive. In the My

Computer illustration, it says Ariel (F:) because my daughter, Haley, has her Little Mermaid game in the CD-ROM drive, and my CD-ROM drive happens to be assigned the letter F.

Fig. 5 My Computer showing the
name of the CD-ROM in
the CD-ROM drive.

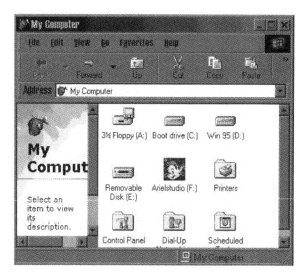

The drives will usually include an A drive, referred to as the floppy drive. This is the drive that houses those square disks that are 3 ½" x 3 ½". Hence the name three-and-a-half-inch-floppy disk.

You will most likely have a CD-ROM drive, that may be labeled D or G or another letter (in my case F), in the My Computer window. These CD-ROM drives house CDs much like audio CDs you can play on a stereo. As a matter of fact, Audio CDs will play in your computer CD drive. All you need are speakers and software that can play the music. Both of which you may already have— especially if you have a new computer. One thing I want to stress is that you should not put a data CD into your stereo CD player. You will blow your speakers if you do. A computer CD-ROM drive can accommodate an audio or a data CD, but a stereo CD player can only accommodate an audio CD. A data CD would be one that does not have music on it. A CD with a game or your ISPs disk are both examples of data CD-ROMs.

REMOVABLE DISK DRIVES

There are a lot of larger removable storage media on the market nowadays that threaten the longevity of the 3 ½" floppy. Some of these drives include Jazz drives, Zip drives, and Superdisks. The latter holds 120 MB, roughly 80 times what a standard floppy holds which is 1.44 MB. The problem with a lot of *removable storage media*, so called because you can actually remove the disk and take it to another computer unlike your hard drive, is that they are not industry standard. Therefore, if another computer doesn't have the same kind of removable storage device, it will not be able to read the disk. As soon as the day comes when there is an industry standard storage media that can hold more data than 1.44MB, the floppy drive as we know it will parish. Actually, these 3 ½" disks are not floppy but firm. However, the term "floppy" still lives on from the days of the 5 ¼" floppy disk that we used in the '80s. These disks were actually somewhat bendable or floppy; they were not as durable as today's floppies and they held a lot less data.

Please allow me to reiterate the principles of this chapter. If you have a CD in the drive, it will show the name of the CD and then the drive letter in My Computer. For example, let's say that you have a CD called America Online. When you put that CD in the drive, you can look at the drive icon in the My Computer window and it will read America Online (D:) (Or whatever drive letter your CD-ROM drive is). Sometimes, an AOL CD will have another name such as Try AOL.

The C drive is the main drive on your computer, and besides the floppy and the CD-ROM, it is usually the only drive on your computer or listed in My Computer. However, That is not always true. You may have a Zip drive or Jazz drive or another type of removable storage. You could have more than one hard drive. Let's just say for now that the C drive is the only one that you have besides a CD-ROM and a floppy drive. The C drive holds all of the files that are on your computer. A tower unit is pictured in **Fig. 6**. The tower physically houses all of your drives. The hard drive is completely inside the tower, so you will not be able to see it from the outside. However, you can see the front of the floppy drive and the CD-ROM drive. To get a glimpse of all of the files on the hard drive, you can double-click on the C drive in the My Computer window. Another way to see all of the files on your computer is to go to the Windows Explorer that will be covered in Chapter 5 *Beyond the Basics*.

Fig. 6 Tower unit. This one has 2 CD-ROM drives and a floppy drive.

Chapter #5

Beyond the Basics

Now that you know basically how the computer works and how to get to the important sections of your computer, we can go online. This is why most people these days, if not nearly everyone, buy a computer anyway isn't it? What's your e-mail address? What's your Web address? It's like if you don't have at least one of these, you're out of the loop. It's kind of neat because the affordable PC has made it possible for nearly every American to have a computer. There have been deals like the CompuServe rebate program where you could buy a computer for $400 and get a $400 rebate. The Microsoft Network had a similar promotion. These deals boil down to essentially a free computer. Inexpensive personal computers have empowered the average person with knowledge and access to virtually anything anybody else has. Only the rich and educated used to be able to obtain valuable information. These were the folks that were online because of educational research requirements or professional job requirements. As an aside, they might go online for pleasure since they had Internet access anyway. Nowadays, with the push of a button (or a mouse) you can access the Library of Congress or get real-time stock quotes. Since knowledge is power, It really gives anybody the potential chance to be successful. I wouldn't say that everybody has an equal shot at life because it still takes money to make money, and if you don't have any, you will probably not get off the ground unless you get discovered by a Hollywood producer or you can throw a baseball 130 mph. The Internet does even the score a little bit though, and it sure has reshaped the way that we do business.

SO YOU WANNA GET ONLINE?

Since you should have an elementary understanding of your computer and how to navigate with your mouse, you should be able to enjoy yourself online. If you haven't picked up the basic skills, you will be ready to throw your computer out the window. You will want to cancel your online service, and you will probably blame technical support for your unhappiness. I won't discuss any particular online service in depth in this book, but most of them have online registration and are pretty intuitive. In other words, you insert their CD into your computer, and if it doesn't start automatically, follow the instructions to kick off the installation and click **Next** or **Ok** or **Continue** or **Yes** through the whole thing and you really can't go wrong. The registration is done in its entirety on the computer, so there is no need to call technical support unless you run into a stumbling block.

Most Internet service providers (ISPs) offer some sort of free trial time. I would encourage a beginner to take several up on the offer to see which one that they like best. There is really no particular ISP that is the best; it is a matter of opinion. That's why it's good to try several because what your friend likes you may hate. That's why they make chocolate and vanilla, so you decide. I also would encourage you to try an easy online service with good 24 x 7 tech support like America Online. You may love this service and want to stay, but even if you don't, they offer a good free trial, the technical support is reliable, and it doesn't get much easier. If you can't navigate on AOL, then you will get very frustrated with any other ISP. America Online has a lot of good content online, and it is competitively priced.

In this book, I will discuss AOL and CompuServe more than any other ISP. The reason is because they are the easiest to use. I started out with America Online when I was a computer novice, and I have subscribed to CompuServe 2000 as well. I have continued to use AOL because they have a knack of putting everything that I need within close range. Even though I can navigate any ISP, I am very short on time. AOL simply saves me time, so I have stuck with it through the years. I still enjoy the convenient ease of use that AOL offers even though I have the knowledge to make any ISP work. As a result, I am more familiar with AOL than any other ISP. In addition, it has evolved into version 6.0; it offers many features that have been lacking from its previous clients. It is finally pretty well rounded, and a lot of functions can be done that AOL members have begged for throughout the years. This shows that AOL listens to its members and tries to incorporate their wants and needs into their software. I can't wait to see what their next version will have in store.

COMPUTERS ARE NOT PERFECT

No matter how easy the software is supposed to be, you may run into problems during setup. There are so many different computers with so many different programs on them that the possible computer configurations are basically infinite. Therefore, no one program can run smoothly on every entire system. Don't let it upset you if everything doesn't go exactly as planned. Like the poet Robert Burns said, The best-laid plans of mice and men often go awry. You see computers are still in their infancy. Think of the automobile in the early 20th century. Computer Science is far from perfect, and the sooner you realize that, the less frustrated you will be when something goes wrong.

When you get done with this book, you may want to look at some of the articles that are referenced in Appendix H *Resources.* **There is a good article in the June 1998 edition of Internet Computing Magazine,** 1*Seeking Windows Compatibility,* **which will give you a more profound understanding of computer incompatibilities.** Most of the time, not only can you order back issues of these magazines, but you can visit their Web site and find articles like this one.

HARDWARE IS HARD AND SOFTWARE IS SOFT

Software is any program that can be installed on your computer. Some software comes preinstalled on your computer as a value-added software package. Other software may come in the form of a compact disk or a 3 ½" floppy disk. Software will install programs that are called *applications*. Programs are merely just instructions written in computer language like English or Spanish but something that a computer can understand. These instructions tell the computer what to do. Your computer really isn't very smart after all you see. It can only do what it is told to do.

In other words, it is only as smart as the applications installed on it. An application would be the result of installing a program. Some examples of applications are Microsoft Office or the Little Mermaid game that my daughter likes.

In contrast, hardware is any tangible component that can be put into your computer or even the external accessories such as a joystick or a mouse. The keyboard is hardware, the CD-ROM drive is hardware (even though you can usually only see the face of it as the rest is set into your computer tower). Other examples of hardware are the modem, sound card, video card, or RAM chips, all residing inside of the tower unit. Because there are so many different combinations of software and hardware, you will frequently hear about incompatibility problems. Maybe you will find out that your modem is not compatible with your ISP or your sound card and your modem conflict. This is just the way it is since computers are far from perfect yet. Sometimes with the wrong combination of hardware and/or software, it is equivalent to a Chevy transmission in a Toyota automobile or a square peg in a round hole or...well you get the idea.

Chapter #6

Something is wrong now whom do I call?

This chapter is intended to give you some basic information about technical support. It is an addendum to Appendix A What *to do and What to Expect When Calling Tech Support*. Something will inevitably go wrong with your computer that will prompt you to call technical support. The question of how to fix the computer may not be as perplexing as the question of who you need to call to fix it.

Do not feel bad if you need to call for help. We all ask for help sometimes believe me. Not too long ago I upgraded my older computer to windows 98. For the life of me I could not get the computer to recognize my Hewlett Packard scanner after the upgrade. After trying everything that I knew to get the scanner installed, I ended up calling HP. The technical support engineer was very knowledgeable and friendly. He explained that I needed an updated driver because the one that originally came with the scanner wasn't compatible with Windows 98. A driver is a little program that makes it possible for the computer to communicate with a certain device such as a scanner. He then ordered a CD for me—problem solved.

I could have easily banged my head against the wall for an entire weekend if I was afraid to ask for help. As it turns out, there was a very simple solution to my problem. Making a call to tech support saved me a lot of time. I was impressed with the caliber of Hewlett Packard's representative, and calling them was a pleasant experience all the way around.

Incidentally, I noticed how smoothly the call went since I knew what he was talking about. When I hung up the phone, I sat there for a minute and thought how awful that call would have probably been, for me and for him, if I had known nothing about computers. I think that he would have charged me for the phone call except that he knew that I understood computers, and he respected that. It did cost me $20 for the CD, but that was nominal since they could have easily charged me several bucks a minute for the phone call also. He told me that he was not going to charge me. You may be thinking that it is discriminatory to only charge people that don't know what they are doing. I mean that's why you are calling tech support in the first place right? That is a valid point for sure, but I'm not sure if he didn't charge me because I could speak his language or if it was that I had a fairly new scanner or that I casually mentioned that I had 3 Hewlett Packard printers. I didn't mention that to brag or anything; I merely mentioned it in passing as in "I have 3 of your printers and 2 scanners, and I have never had to do so much as update a driver until now." Then I told him that I love Hewlett Packard products because of the hassle-free enjoyment I have had using them. Okay, I was brown-nosing a little bit with the last remark, but I wasn't lying and it probably saved me about $30.

THE LESS YOU KNOW THE MORE YOU'LL OWE

It is likely that the less you know about computers the more you will be charged for tech support. If nothing more, the technician is going to need to take more time with you if you don't know your way around the computer. If it is not free tech support that you are dealing with, you will probably fair better with a per-incident charge if you are a beginner. A lot of companies operate this way. For example, it will cost you $35 per incident no matter what. Some companies have a deal like $35 flat or $3 per minute. If it takes the technician 5 minutes to get you into Windows

Explorer, the per-minute-charge deal is going to end up costing you big bucks.

Furthermore, there may be times when a company will charge a novice and not charge someone who seems computer savvy. You have to look at it from a corporate point of view. If the tech support is free, it costs companies big bucks. Some technical support departments just charge a nominal fee, but it is merely enough to pay the engineer and put a few bucks in the corporate kiddy. But whatever the case, tech support departments get pretty sick of people that have to ask where the Start button is. And believe me that when tech support is free, the executives don't like it either because that nonsense makes for longer calls and thus costs the company more money. Just thought I would point this out because it is further motivation for you to learn the basics at least. On the other hand, don't be afraid to call for help no matter what your knowledge level. I mean it is really the companies problem if it costs them money and not yours. The experience will be a lot better for both you and the person on the other end of the phone if you know where your Start button is though.

When I took technical support phone calls, many people I talked to intensified their problem before they finally decided to call. I don't know how many times I've heard "I should have called you sooner." Some people even went so far as to delete all of their important files before calling me. By the time I got them, I could do nothing to resurrect their files, but if they had called sooner, they wouldn't have lost anything important. I know that it seems like an admission of weakness to call tech support. Actually, it takes an emotionally strong and secure person to ask for help.

TECH SUPPORT IS TO SOLVE YOUR PROBLEM

If you do call technical support and the experience isn't going as well as I described with Hewlett Packard, try not to take it too personally. If the tech support is free, just hang up and call back. In any given organization, you will usually find new people that aren't that knowledgeable about their line of work. You will also find old timers who will know all of the ins and outs of their profession. Also, there will be everyone in between the newbie and the old timer. Chances are that if you get someone the first time that didn't seem that knowledgeable, he or she was new to the company. Chances are that if you call back again, you will get someone with some tenure that can solve your problem.

There is no excuse for poor customer service, and downright rudeness is obviously wrong. However, try not to be too offended if the technician that you talk to isn't bubbling over with enthusiasm. These people have a difficult job. A lot of times their job is repetitious; the other times the problems that arise require some deep thought and problem solving capabilities. It is hard for a company to find a good technician, with good analytical skills, that also has a bubbly personality. Usually the two virtues don't coincide.

I'm not excusing any unfriendliness or condescending words that may exude out of a tech support persons mouth. I'm merely informing you that they are usually under a fair amount of pressure; they usually have many guidelines that they have to adhere to such as the amount of time that they can spend with each customer. That particular metric may not exist if you are paying for support, however. In addition, tech reps deal with a lot of monotony; they talk to perhaps dozens of people a day that are computer novices, and it is necessary to repeat the same elementary steps over and over again. Therefore, as long as they aren't mean, and of course as long as they are knowledgeable, try to concentrate on getting your problem solved and don't worry too much if you wouldn't vote for them in a congeniality contest. I mean I think that the most important thing is that the person that you talk to is knowledgeable. You call because you want your problem solved in a reasonable amount of time right?

MAKE SURE YOU CAN CALL SOMEBODY

Now I'm finally done with that long-winded introduction to this chapter. Like I said, for more on that note read Appendix A at the end of this book. What I want to tell you now is how to tell whom you should call when something goes wrong with your computer. An important thing to mention is that you want to make sure that you have someone to call. In other words, if you have a choice, make sure that you have a clear line to technical support; make sure that you have a clear understanding of your technical support options. If you are buying a new computer, make sure that there is someone you can call if things go wrong. Find out what hours they are open, how much the cost will be, and other such details that pertain to your warranty. Most importantly, if you buy a new computer, make sure somebody is available to help you out if things go wrong. This advice is never truer if you are a computer novice. The exception may be if you know a computer expert that can be at your beck and call if your system goes belly up. If you are making a new computer purchase, you have a right to get an answer to all of these questions—and any other questions or concerns that you may have. If the manufacturer is unable or unwilling to answer these types of questions for you, go somewhere else. There is too much competition in the computer arena to settle for a deal that leaves a bad taste in your mouth.

If you bought an inexpensive used computer, or you inherited a hand-me-down computer, you probably won't have a choice as far as technical support. However, if you do purchase a used computer, check and see if there is a transferable warranty. Moreover, I would take that factor into serious consideration if I was going to buy a used computer; technical support or not could definitely sway my decision to make the purchase or not. If you buy a new computer, I would not settle for one with no tech support options just to save a couple of hundred dollars—it will most likely end up costing you a lot more in the long run than you saved. For one thing, if there is no one you can call to walk you through fixing the computer via the telephone, you will likely need to go to the trouble of disconnecting all of the wiring and actually bringing the tower unit into a repair shop. However, there are general tech support options available. They will troubleshoot your system over the telephone no matter what brand of computer you have, and it doesn't matter if it's under warranty or not. Of course you are usually going to pay for these, so be sure and get the pricing straight from the start. In a lot of cases, you will probably end up paying a lot less than if you brought the system into a shop. And, you won't have to wait several days or more to get back up and running. One way to find these is to go online and visit a popular search engine. For your search criteria, type in **tech support** or **technical support**. One that I know of offhand is Webhelp.com, the Internet's real-time, human-assisted search service. It can be found at **http://www.webhelp.com.** There are some more links that follow that will help you find general tech support and a lot of them do offer free support.

PC WORLD magazine conducted a *best and the worst* study of fee-based and free technical support. The excerpts below convey some of what they had to say about technical support operations. See **Appendix H**, *Resources*, to find out exactly where you can find this entire article.

2*"Internet support usually falls into one of three categories: forums, expert advice sites, and knowledge bases. Forums are bulletin boards where people post questions and answers for each other. You can also post a question at an expert advice site, but only one person will respond—an "expert" responsible for answering questions. At a knowledge base, you can search an online database to find answers to specific questions. A site needn't be limited to a single approach—NoWonder.com, for example, offers both forums and expert advice, while About.com uses all three methods."*

ask-a-tech.org

dialatech.com

32bit.com

About.com

Computing.net

EHow.com

Goofy Guys.com

My Help Desk.com

No Wonder.comPC Support Center

Virtual Dr.com

ExpertsExchange.com-Uses a point system to ration the number of questions you can ask.

ExpertCity.com-Charges for information but claims that it can respond almost immediately as well as provide more than one solution.

Askme.com-Offers a mix of free and fee-based services.
This site was formerly Xpertsite.com.

Service911.com-Offers a mix of free and fee-based services.

"You're most likely to find the right answer at a forum site such as 32bit.com, About.com, Computing.net, NoWonder.com, or VirtualDr.com. The community spirit of a forum increases the likelihood that you'll get a variety of opinions and more than one way to solve a problem, and that good advice from one person will correct bad advice from someone else.

You don't get that kind of give-and-take experience from an expert advice site, where only one person reads your question, and only you read his or her answer. The quality of these sites—About.com, GoofyGuys.com, NoWonder.com, and PCSupport.com—depends entirely on the quality of the professionals hired or, in some cases, the volunteers selected to answer your questions."

You will probably have some kind of online service that you will use on your computer. Things will invariably happen on your computer that will raise the question: Is this a computer problem or is it my ISP's problem? Sometimes, there is a fine line between one and the other. You may be tempted to call your ISP over your computer manufacturer because perhaps it's free, or the hold time is less, or the hours are more convenient. If you want to call just to see if the problem belongs to the manufacturer or the ISP, that's fine, but just don't expect them to fix it if it is a general computer problem. Conversely, don't expect your manufacturer to fix the problem if it is related to your ISP. There is such a fine line between just what problem may belong to who that you may find yourself being bounced back and forth between your ISP's tech support and the computer manufacturer's tech support. This may not be entirely either parties fault. Human nature is going to dictate that they take the path of least resistance, so each company will be inclined to refer you to the other if there is any doubt whatsoever. It may be helpful in certain situations to see if one of the technical support departments would set up a conference call where you can talk to both your manufacturer and ISP simultaneously.

There is so much ambiguity in the tech support arena that it is an important thing to mention in a book such as this one. One of the main reasons why it can be confusing in diagnosing a problem is that your ISP will use a Web browser. If they use Microsoft Internet Explorer, that is really a Microsoft product. If there is a problem with the browser, the question can come up as to whether your computer manufacturer should help you fix it, your ISP, or Microsoft themselves. If it is Windows 98, the answer will likely be the computer manufacturer because the browser is integrated into Windows 98 so tightly that in order to fix it, if it is badly damaged, Windows usually will need to be reinstalled. If the computer is running Windows 98, but it is no longer under warranty, Microsoft will be the company that you will need to call if you have a serious browser problem. Either that or you can pay for support from the manufacturer if you have a brand-name computer even if it is out of warranty.

Confusing the matter even more, the same exact symptoms can mean a bad browser or about a dozen other things. It is hard to confirm that the browser is bad without going through a long list of troubleshooting procedures first. At that point, the browser may be deemed to be damaged, and from there a lot of things may need to be tried before it may be discovered that Windows is hosed.

With Windows 95, an ISP will have a little more leeway on what they can do and what they can't as far as the Web browser. Therefore, they may be able to help you with a more serious browser problem because the Microsoft Internet Explorer browser can be removed safely in Windows 95 unlike in Windows 98. However, if they help you through a complete delete and reinstall of the browser, and you still can't get to the Web, or if the browser will not uninstall properly, your ISP will likely refer you to Microsoft. They did make Windows and the Web browser, so it eventually boils down to their problem. Your ISP's software works hand-in-hand with the Windows operating system and everything is somewhat intermingled. Therefore, if you have problems with Windows, or some peculiarities, it is likely that the ISP's software will not work properly. Other applications may work fine unless Windows is badly damaged. The reason why it may work that way is because your ISP uses the modem, sound card, and Web browser. Those items require more resources from your computer than anything else on your computer; if your computer has an Achilles heel, it will surely be found when any of those items are being used—and especially all three. Chances are that no other application on your computer uses the modem, sound card, and Web browser simultaneously except your ISP.

If you still have Windows 95 these days, chances are your computer isn't under warranty anymore. If you need technical support for Windows, you will either have to pay the manufacturer or Microsoft, and it might as well be Microsoft since it is really their product. If the problem is with the hardware, that would fall under the realm of the manufacturer; Microsoft would only be responsible for Windows and Microsoft Internet Explorer (Or any other Microsoft software such as Microsoft Publisher). Your ISP would probably like to help you further with some problems that are really Microsoft issues. It is not just out of incivility that they won't help you with certain things. It is important to understand that they are legally bound not to cross certain lines with the operating system because they are not licensed to do so. Microsoft would need to grant every employee in your ISPs tech support a license to perform certain functions that only Microsoft engineers, that work for Microsoft, can do. An ISP can be sued, and lose, by both Microsoft and the customer if they start fiddling with the guts of the Windows operating system itself.

REAL WORLD EXAMPLES OF TECH SUPPORT SCENARIOS

An obvious scenario is that your computer won't even start. If this is the case, your problem lies with Windows—A product made by Microsoft. Therefore, if you have no one else to call for support, you will need to call Microsoft for this issue. A new computer will come preloaded with Windows, as well as a lot of other software most likely, so the manufacturer of your computer will be responsible for anything wrong with the software or hardware—including Windows. If your computer is out of warranty, you may need to call Microsoft if your computer won't even boot up. I won't print any tech support numbers in this book because by the time this book goes into print, any number that I put in here would likely be changed. Many tech support companies change their numbers frequently. A technician for a large hardware manufacturer told me that they had to discontinue one of their support line numbers because they had enough of the "where is the Start button" calls. He proceeded to give me an obscure 800 number that was a free tech support call. I gave that number out to select customers if I felt that they at least knew the basics, had a need to talk to this company, and could follow instructions. So be nice to your tech support person. Remember that you can catch more flies with honey than vinegar. If you need a phone number though, try 1-800-555-1212. That number is for the national 800 number directory assistance. It's not likely to be going away anytime soon either. That number has been the same for as long as I can remember.

You may feel that your ISP, or their software, made your computer unable to start up. Although this is possible, it is very unlikely that it is their fault. You may want to call and see if there is a known issue with your particular computer. For example, it was known that installing America Online version 5.0 would make a Gateway Astro unable to start up normally. Customers had to obtain an operating system patch to solve the problem. Thus, while it was really a Gateway problem, America Online's tech support was able to tell its members to call Gateway and obtain the patch. Of course because of that incident, and because of some isolated problems with AOL 5.0, the press blew it out of proportion. Even a year or more after AOL 5.0 came out, many people thought that it would damage their computer. It turns out that in nearly every case when AOL seemed to do some damage to a computer, there was a good reason for it. Most of the time when AOL 5.0 would cause a problem, save the Gateway Astro and another proprietary brand or two, the person had some kind of Windows configuration that wasn't even supported by Microsoft—such as certain networking components installed. If the Windows configuration isn't even supported by its own maker, meaning that Microsoft doesn't guarantee it to work properly, then it is very likely that any software installation is going to have unpredictable results—including making the computer unbootable.

Logically, especially with an ISP as large as AOL, you have to look at a problem from a birds-eye view. If you think that software has hosed your system, try and find out what effects it has had on other people's computers. If your system is the only one that it hosed, then it's not the software that is the problem—it's your computer. In AOL's case, if their software was truly full of bugs, it would have messed up 20 million member's computers. America Online version 5.0 had an adverse effect on maybe something like 20,000 computers—including the Gateway Astro: You do the math.

If there isn't a widespread problem such as the Gateway Astro example, and you still feel that your ISP's software rendered your computer unbootable, you may still want to call them because there may be something peculiar about your computer that they need to know about in order to warn people in the future that have that same peculiarity. Don't expect your ISP to help you if the computer will not start because they will probably refer you to your manufacturer no matter what the circumstance. Let's say that you have no strange hardware or software on your computer, and there's no known issues about your specific system. If software crashes your computer, it is probably because there was some instability in the Windows operating system environment to begin with. In other words, the computer may have been about to crash anyway. The hard drive may be worn out, the Windows Registry may be corrupt, or a number of other things. Something would have probably gone wrong with your computer in the near future anyway, and the software installation may have brought that problem to the surface.

America Online version 6.0 seemed to bring a whole new set of problems but the release of 6.0 was reminiscent of when AOL 5.0 came out. There may have been some problems with version 6.0 during the preview stages, but I believe that they have finally worked out the kinks with later builds of the client. However, America Online version 6.0 seems to infiltrate all of the cracks and crevices of a computer, so underlying problems are more likely to show up than with most other programs. Think of all of the buttons on a universal remote control for a TV or for your remote control. Do you use every single button? Chances are that you use maybe half a dozen of the buttons and that's it, but there may be dozens of buttons in some cases. You could have problems with your television or some of the components that you have hooked up to your TV, but you wouldn't even realize it unless you tried to use some of those obscure buttons on your remote control. Figuratively speaking, AOL 6.0 uses all of the buttons on your computer, so problems may come to the surface that no other program will bring out.

Chapter #7

E-mail info

The beauty of e-mail is that it is free. Well, the United States Post office will probably try to get their piece of the pie eventually, but at this point in time, you can send e-mail around the world and receive e-mail from anywhere in the world for free. E-mail is really the best thing since the light bulb, and it is probably the main reason why many of you are going to want to get online or have gotten online already. It's not only cool to have an e-mail address, but it's almost become uncouth not to have one. When you are chitchatting at a party, you will want to boast your e-mail address; you will probably feel like a square peg if all of your friends swap their addresses and you have to sit there in silence.

E-mail fortunately is pretty intuitive, so you don't have to be a computer geek to use it. However, there are some general things that you should know about e-mail. First of all, some online services, like America Online and CompuServe 2000, have proprietary e-mail that means that other mail programs won't work in conjunction with them. In other words, you can only use the e-mail programs that are built into these services. This is not necessarily bad, but some people have gotten used to their own mail programs and they don't like this limitation. However, CompuServe 2000 has recently made it possible to use other mail programs, and I suspect that AOL may follow since this is in such demand.

TYPES OF E-MAIL PROGRAMS

Some of these other mail programs include Microsoft's Outlook, Netscape's mail called Messenger, and Eudora. There are a few other ones around, but these 3 are by far the most widely used. Some other e-mail programs include Pegasus and Juno. Netscape's new mail program is called Web Mail, included in their version 6.0 browser. Most standard ISPs will integrate well with a 3rd

party mail program. Remember that AOL, CompuServe, and Prodigy are really defined as online services and a standard ISP is something like Bellsouth.net, Earthlink or "Mom & Pop's ISP." Online services include a lot of online content that is specific to these services and a portal to the Internet. Whereas an ISP is usually a direct connection to the Internet and that's it accept for e-mail. They usually aren't as user-friendly as an online service, and sometimes they don't even have an integrated e-mail program or the one that they do have is substandard. This means that you have to get your own 3rd party e-mail program that is more difficult because it is another piece of software that you have to learn. In this context, these programs, are referred to as 3rd party programs because they don't belong to the ISP and they don't belong to you, but it is another company that made the software. To compose e-mail on AOL, all you do is click on **Write** on the Toolbar and type your message and click on **Send Now…** it just doesn't get much easier than that folks. More on e-mail in specific online services is discussed in *Compquest Volume 2* Chapter 18, *E-mail.*

HOW DO YOU ACTUALLY SEND IT?

E-mail is similar to traditional mail called "snail mail" because you put whom the mail is going to, a subject line, and you have the content or the body of the letter itself. There are some differences that are inherent with electronic technology versus paper technology. For instance, you may not put a subject line on snail mail per se. However, it is likely your subject line would be in the first sentence or two anyway. Such as Dear Reader: Let me tell you about what I did last summer... The subject line for e-mail in this case could be "What I did last summer," and with snail mail or e-mail you would go on and tell your friend about all the exotic vacations that you took to Africa or New Guinea—or wish you did. You don't have to put a subject line on an e-mail either, but you usually want to give your intended recipient some kind of clue as to just what the mail is about. Otherwise, your e-mail will automatically say 'no subject' for the subject line and that is what your reader will see before they open their e-mail. You need to type in the e-mail address of the person that you are sending the mail to and not the person's real name. In some cases a person may have their real name for their e-mail address, and in that case of course you would put their real name in for the e-mail address.

ATTACHMENTS AND EMBEDS AND OTHER E-MAIL FEATURES

An illustration of an America Online e-mail form is shown in **fig. 7**. All e-mail forms follow the same principles really. You will notice the SEND TO box where you type the person's e-mail address that you want to send the mail to. The subject line we already talked about. You can put any-thing there or nothing at all. The subject line can be "Hi howya doin?" or whatever. Then you just type your message in the larger window at the bottom, and when you are done, click SEND NOW in the upper-right corner. If you wanted to attach a file, you would click the Attachments button in the lower-left corner. Attachments are beyond the scope of this book. However, they are covered in detail in *Compquest Volume 2*, such as in Chapter 19, *File Attachments*. All I will mention on this subject now is that you can send pictures directly in e-mail with some e-mail programs like AOL or CompuServe 2000. However, the recipient of your e-mail would need to have the same mail program to see an ***embedded picture*** otherwise you would need to send the picture as a *file attachment* that must be downloaded and read by an application (program) on the recipients computer. The application that is needed to open a file attachment is dependent on the attachment's file extension. All files have a 3-letter extension that distinguishes them. Check out Appendix J, *File Extensions* for a list of these and the applications that are usually associated with them.

Fig. 7 AOL e-mail form.

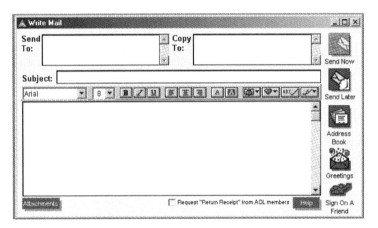

Illustrated in **fig. 8** is an Outlook Express e-mail form. Outlook is a popular e-mail program that is produced by Microsoft. Notice how similar the basic workings are to the AOL form. With Outlook you have a To box instead of a Send To box like on AOL. You have a subject line and a large message window at the bottom. When you're done, you click Send in the upper-left corner with Outlook. One thing to realize is that you do not need to include your e-mail address anywhere when you send e-mail. The system will automatically fill it in for you. This is definitely an improvement over snail mail where we are used to writing a return address on the envelope.

There is such a thing as a *signature file* that is possible to have with America Online version 5.0 and above, CompuServe 2000 version 5.0, Outlook Express and most of the other 3rd party e-mail programs. A signature file is a closing statement that can be programmed into every e-mail that you send out. It will normally appear at the bottom of your e-mail automatically once it is programmed in. This could be your real name, your name and occupation or title, or it can be whatever you want within reason. Sometimes, people even have a little graphic in their signature file that represents them. This is equivalent to the way a company logo represents a company. The graphic part of a signature file may or may not be able to be seen by your recipient. Like I said before, you can only embed graphics with certain e-mail programs, and they can only be seen in certain e-mail programs. The recipient needs to have one of these mail systems to see the picture or graphic. In other words, if you have AOL you can send pictures to another AOL member directly in e-mail. If you have AOL, you can send pictures in e-mail directly to a CompuServe 2000 member. If you have CompuServe 2000, you can send AOL members pictures embedded in e-mail. You can embed a graphic and send it to whoever you want to, but if they don't use one of these systems, or a mail system that supports embedded graphics, they will see text that tells them that there is supposed to be a picture there but they will be unable to see the picture.

fig. 8 Outlook Express e-mail form.

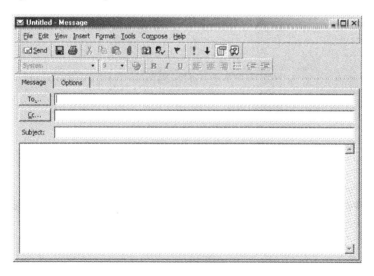

Chapter #8

What is the Internet and how do I get there?

The Internet is a vast place that could be compared to the universe. It is vast, no one owns the Internet, and there are few rules and even fewer people or agencies that govern any rules that there are. The Internet is actually composed of every single online service, ISP, and Web page in existence. The *World Wide Web* (WWW) is part of the Internet. The WWW is composed of what has become millions of Web pages that are somewhat linked together—hence the name Web. You need to have a connection to the Internet and a Web browser in order to view Web pages. The two most popular Web browsers are the Microsoft Internet Explorer and Netscape Navigator. A Web browser is merely a program that can read Web pages. Web pages are written in a computer language that is called *HTML* (Hypertext Markup Language) or some variation thereof. A Web browser translates that language, so the Web page appears as you see it instead of a bunch of programming code. A Web browser is not a connection, but if you have a connection to the Internet, you can browse Web pages with a browser.

WHAT'S IN A NAME?

A Web address usually goes something like www.whatever.com. You really have to be living in a cave not to see and hear of these addresses all of the time on TV and the radio these days. On a user-friendly service, such as America Online or CompuServe 2000, you can simply type this address in the long white bar at the top of your screen (under all the little picture icons at the very top), and either hit the **Enter** key on your keyboard or click **GO** to the right of the white line to invoke your Web browser and bring up a Web page. Since these services are friendlier than most, all you need to do is type in www.microsoft.com to go to Microsoft's Web site. However, on many ISPs it may be necessary to type the full address. In that example, the full address would be http://www.microsoft.com; it might need to be typed that way in order to actually reach a Web page. HTTP stands for *Hypertext Transfer Protocol*, a technical term that simply is a standard protocol for Web pages.

Because a browser is not an Internet connection, if you want to get to the Web by clicking on the Internet Explorer icon on the Desktop, it may be necessary to connect to your ISP first. America Online and CompuServe 2000 use Internet Explorer as their integrated Web browser, meaning that when you go to the Internet on these services, you are actually using the Microsoft Explorer Web browser that is installed already in Windows. It may look a little bit different, but it's the same browser. The only changes to the browser are essentially cosmetic: It will have an AOL logo in the upper-right corner instead of the Microsoft logo. If you use either one of these services and you want to get to the Internet specifically by clicking on the Internet Explorer icon, you will need to connect to AOL or CompuServe 2000 first, minimize it, and then click on the Explorer icon. The reason why it must be done this way is that you are establishing your connection to the Internet by dialing into AOL or CompuServe 2000. When you minimize the program, it enables you to see the Desktop where all of the icons are. From that standpoint, you can click on the Internet Explorer icon. Since your ISP is running in the background, the browser will enable you to read Web pages. The browser is not a connection though, so you cannot dial into the Internet with it or establish your initial Internet connection.

MINIMIZE FRUSTRATION AND MAXIMIZE PRO-DUCTIVITY

Minimize a program by clicking on the little minus (-) sign in the upper-right corner of your screen. The **X** in the upper-right will close a window entirely, and the square, that sometimes looks like a little square within a square, will make the window smaller. When it looks like a square within a square, the window will be full size. When it just looks like a larger square, the window will be shrunken a bit but won't be completely minimized. So if your window ever appears smaller than it should, like it is pushed part of the way off the screen, try clicking the square in the upper-right corner and it may return the screen to normal size. If you minimize a program by clicking on the minus sign, it will go down to the *Taskbar*, the line that is kind of the extension of the Start button that usually runs along the bottom of the screen. To the right of the Taskbar is the Systray or *System Tray* where you will find the computer clock and usually a megaphone icon that will allow you to adjust the speaker volume. If you have minimized your program and it is sitting on the Taskbar, it will appear as a rectangular-shaped icon. All you need to do in order to bring the minimized program back up to a full screen is to click on it once on the Taskbar.

Missing Windows from the Desktop

TIP If a program window or a folder seems to have just vanished off of your screen, the most likely cause is that you've changed your video resolution. It can be due to several other reasons, however. Right-click on the taskbar, select either the Cascade Windows or Tile Windows (Horizontally or Vertically) option, and the window may reappear. You may need to resize your windows after that is done.

KEY WORDS AND GO WORDS IN OTHER WORDS

Specifically, on America Online the keyboard command to bring up an address line where you can type a Web address is **CTRL+K** (Press your **CTRL** key in the lower left corner of your keyboard and then press the letter **K** at the same time). You can type an address on this line instead of typing it in the white bar at the top of the screen. On the same line you could also type an AOL keyword (that's why it is the letter K and not another letter—K=keyword) such as Help. So if someone said go to keyword Help, you would press the **CTRL+K**, and on the keyword line type in the word 'Help' without quotes and then just click on **GO** or hit the **Enter** key on your keyboard. CompuServe 2000 is similar except instead of keywords it has Go words. Therefore, to bring up a Go line you would press **CTRL+G** and then type in the word 'Help' without quotes and click on **GO** or hit your **Enter** key on your keyboard to get to that place. These words are specific to these services, and it is easier than going to a Web page because instead of having to type in an entire address, you need to only type in one word. To get a list of all of these words that help you navigate around these services quickly, after pressing **CTRL+K** on AOL, just click on where it says **keyword list**. On CompuServe after pressing **CTRL+G** click on where it says **go word list**.

GET TO KNOW YOUR WEB SITE

One thing to keep in mind: When you are using an online service these keywords or go words take you to places that you can only get to on these services. In other words, they were put there by these services, and they are maintained by these specific services. However, When you go to a Web site you are totally out of the realm of their parameters. The only exception is if you go to a Web site that is run by an online service such as www.aol.com or www.compuserve.com. Other than that, if you go to lets say www.ripoff.com and buy a product and never receive it, your online

service is not going to be able to do anything about it because they probably have no affiliation with the Web site that you visited. To rephrase this: America Online provides access to the World Wide Web. On the World Wide Web there are literally millions of Web sites. Each site is usually independent of one another, so if they are selling something, they are a business just like a bricks and mortar store like Home Depot or Target. To hold your ISP or online service responsible for a bad experience that you had on the WWW would be the equivalent of calling your
cable company and expecting some aggressive action from them because you had a bad experience with some business that you saw advertised on a commercial. After all, you saw a commercial on your TV that is brought to you by your cable company. In most cases, the cable company will not have any direct affiliation with any of the companies that run commercials other than the cable company is paid to run the advertisements. Most likely your online service will not have any affiliation at all with most Web sites on the World Wide Web.

Therefore, if you have a beef with a Web site, you will need to take it up with that site individually. You can usually write an e-mail to the Webmaster of a Web site. For example, address your e-mail to webmaster@thedomain.com or **Webmaster@thesiteinquestion.com** if you see no other way on the site to reach anybody. However, Web sites will usually have a button to click on that says Contact Us, Customer Service, or something similar.

SAFETY AND SECURITY ON THE WEB

E-commerce has become very widespread, and far and wide it is very safe to shop on the Web and you will usually get what you order. It might be just as safe or safer even than shopping the traditional way, and most people that sell something on the Web have a secure server. This means that if you enter your credit card information online, it is encrypted such that it is virtually impossible for anybody to hack their way into your information. But if they do, instead of seeing your credit card information they will see indecipherable computer code or it will be scrambled in some way. Web sites that offer a secure server usually have a Web address on the page where you will be asked for your information that starts with https. Remember how the entire address of a Web page starts with http? Well, https or specifically the 's' stands for secure. If you go to www.amazon.com and click on this link and click on that link and you order something, you will notice that when you are on the page that asks for your credit card number, the address that displays in your Web browsers address bar will start with https. In addition, with some browsers, you will see a little icon of a padlock in the lower left or right hand corner that also denotes a secure site. The padlock will be open on a non-secure site; it will be shut on a secure site.

This sort of information and some more advanced information about Web browsers constitutes an entirely separate chapter. See the next chapter, Chapter 9 *More About Browsers and the Internet*, for more information about Web browsers and the Internet.

A good magazine article that I ran across is 3*Your First Time Online—What To Expect When You're On The 'Net*. Check out Appendix H, *Resources*, to find out where you can find this article.

Chapter #9

More Info About Browsers and the Internet

WORRY ABOUT YOUR CASH NOT YOUR CACHE

You have probably heard the terms Cache or History or Temporary Internet files and then again maybe not. But what they relate to is your Web browser. There are 3 folders on your computer that store a trail of where you have been on the Internet: *History, Cookies*, and *Temporary Internet Files*. Your Web browser stores information and graphics about the Web sites that you've visited in these folders. More accurately, a list of the WWW addresses that have been visited is stored in the History folder; text and graphics from Web pages that you have visited are stored in the Temporary Internet Files folder. Cookies are files that are transferred to your computer from certain Web sites; their main purpose is that they are used to personalize Web sites.

Generally, there will be no reason to worry about your cache file unless you are trying to track down where someone has been going on the Internet. Theoretically, you can open up the individual files in the Temporary Internet Files folder and see a Web page that you've visited before while you are offline. This may have its advantages because you don't have to be online to do this. However, the page will only be as updated as the last time that you actually went there on the Internet. In addition, Internet Explorer 5.0 and above offers the option to download Web pages for offline reading. You can even save an entire Web page with graphics and all. Using Internet Explorer, when you are on the Web page

that you want to save, click on **File** at the top left and choose **Save As....**
Type in a name that you will recognize where it says File name, and where
it says Save as type:, choose Web Page Complete. This will save a file on
your hard drive that has the entire Web page that you were looking at with
graphics and all. As a matter of fact, With IE 5.0 and above there are four
options under the File>Save As option as far as saving Web pages. This is a
welcome change from older versions of Internet Explorer. *Web page complete* saves the text in one file, and another file holds all the pictures. *Web
Archive, single file* makes one single file for the text and graphics. *Web
page, HTML only*, saves just the HTML that will be the text without formatting, and *Text File* is just what it sounds like; it saves the Web page as
a text file. Appendix C, *How to View Web Pages Offline*, will tell you
exactly how to do these operations. Incidentally, there are shortcut keys
that you can use for Internet Explorer much like shortcut keys in
Windows. A list of these can be found in Appendix G, *Internet Explorer
Keyboard Shortcuts*

Fig. 9   Web page complete selection shown
         for the Save as type drop-down list.

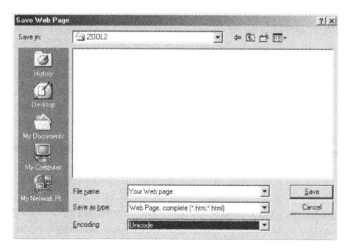

The cache enables Web pages to load more quickly when you return to a Web site because some of the artwork is already on your computer so it doesn't have to load everything directly from the site itself. Ironically, if the cache gets too full it can keep you from getting to the Web at all because it will attempt to load all of the files in the Temporary Internet folder before even loading the Web page. If the Temporary Internet Files folder is huge, it will just cause the computer to hang, meaning that the mouse pointer will remain an hourglass, and the Web page will never even come up.

There is another folder called Cookies that stores cookies that your computer receives from Web sites. Contrary to popular belief, cookies are not viruses and in most cases they are fairly benign. However, some people do find them obtrusive because in some cases they can track everywhere that you go on the Internet. Cookies basically enable a Web site to personalize itself to you. Sometimes, when you return to a Web site, you will see a message that says something like "Welcome **your name** thank you for coming back." The way that they know your name is because the first time that you visited the Web site it planted a cookie on your computer in the Cookies folder. There is a way to set your browser to warn you before accepting cookies, but it is really a nuisance because every time a site wants to plant a cookie a message pops up on your screen asking whether you want to accept a cookie or not. If you click No, you won't go any further on that Web site anyway. So in a way a cookie can be like a key that you need to accept to go any deeper into a Web site.

SO YOUR PROBABLY GOING TO ASK HOW TO GET RID OF THESE FILES RIGHT?

Here's how you do it:

Click on **Start** point to **Programs** then click **Windows Explorer**. Scroll down with the vertical scroll bar and look on the left-hand side until you see a folder called Windows. Click on the plus sign (+) on the left-hand side of the Windows folder and underneath Windows you should be able to locate the History folder. The History will appear to have a little blue dot on it, but it is really a tiny globe. Double-click on the **History**, and it will bring up all of its contents on the right-hand side (**fig. 10**). All you need to do from here is click on **Edit** in the far upper-left corner of your screen on the Toolbar and click on **Select All**. You will notice that all the files will highlight. Make sure that the highlighted files are actually contents of the History! It will say History in the address bar at the top portion of the window, and that's how you will know that you have the correct files. Then, click on **File** in the far upper-left corner and click on **Delete**. Click **Yes** to delete them all and then **Yes to all** if that option comes up. Then, scroll down a little bit more and locate the Temporary Internet Files folder and double-click on it. That will bring up all of the contents of the Temporary Internet Files on the right-hand side. Just simply repeat the instructions, the same way as you cleared the history, to get rid of them.

Fig. 10 History file shown in Windows Explorer.

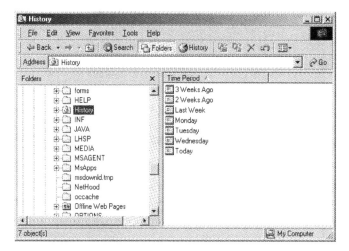

If you scroll back up, you will see a folder called Cookies. You can delete those if you want to in the same manner. Sometimes, you will get a message when deleting the contents of any one of these folders that says, "Cannot delete... access denied. Make sure the disk is not full or write protected..." or something to that effect. If you get this message, it will usually delete everything except a file that you are not supposed to delete anyway. If a file will not delete, it is usually a system file. A system file is one that Windows needs to function, and if you delete it, you can really screw things up. This might happen particularly with the Cookies folder. If it does, don't worry about it because it will still delete everything that should be deleted. You will probably still see one file left which is the one that I am talking about that needs to stay in there. If you try and delete it, you will get a message something like: "This is a system folder if you delete it this program or other programs may not function properly." It will give you a prompt like "Are you sure you want to delete it?" If you say "Yes" to this, don't say that I didn't warn you. However, the message will more than likely be "Cannot delete _____. Access is denied. The source file may be in use" or something to that effect; if the message is similar or the same as that one, it will not let you delete the file anyway.

Sometimes, in rare cases, you will not be able to get to the Web anymore because of a corrupt cache. It may not be that the contents of the cache files have corrupted, but it is the entire folders themselves that store all of the contents. Therefore, the entire folders need to be deleted. The following is a little technical in nature, but in extreme cases it may be necessary to go to DOS mode and delete these entire folders that will delete the folders and all of their contents. These instructions in this chapter or that you may find throughout the entire book are at your own risk! If you do not feel completely comfortable doing these things, or maybe even if you do, it would be advisable to check with your computer manufacturer's technical support and/or Microsoft if you have any problems related to Windows, the Web browser, or accessing the Web. The following instructions are merely there for instructional purposes only.

HOW TO CLEAR YOUR CACHE USING THE DOS MODE METHOD

Click on **Start** and point to **Programs** and choose **MS DOS prompt.** If you don't see this listing click on **Start** then choose **Run.** On the run line type **command** and click **Ok.** This will bring a DOS window up, and you will be at what is called a DOS command prompt. It will look like this: C:\Windows\Desktop as shown in **fig. 11.**

Fig. 11 Dos Window

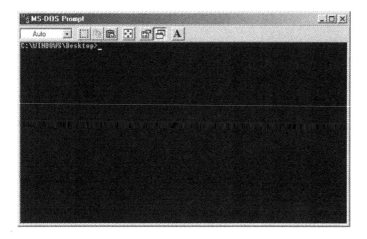

You want to be at the C:\Windows prompt to type some commands, so if it says C:\Windows\Desktop, type **cd..** and hit the **Enter** key on your key-board and it will take you up one directory level to the C:\Windows prompt. Type in the following line exactly as shown with the spaces: **del-tree history cookies tempor*** The "*" is the shift of the 8 key by the way, and it is called an asterisk. After you type in that line, hit the **Enter** key and it will say "delete the directory history and all of its subdirectories?" Y/N? This means Yes or No, so you want to hit the letter **Y** on your keyboard for Yes and hit the **Enter** key. Follow suit when it asks you for the other 2 files, and when it's done you will have completely cleared out your cache. After that, type in **exit** and hit the **Enter** key on your keyboard and it will close the DOS window or just click the "**X**" in the upper-right corner to close the DOS window. So if you have been surfing the porno sites and you want to ensure that nobody finds out about it, this is the method that you want to use because it will clear out everything.

Another way to get into DOS by the way is to click **Start** then choose **Shut down** and click on the circle to put a dot where it says **Restart in MS-DOS mode** then click **Ok**. This will restart your computer in DOS mode which might take a minute or two, but it is supposed to come up to the C:\Windows prompt just the same where you can follow the directions stated before. To restart the computer while in DOS mode, Type in **win** and hit the **Enter** key or press the **CTRL+ALT** keys at the same time and hit the **DELETE** key twice while still holding down the other 2 keys. You will not have the option to restart the computer in DOS mode if you have Windows Me or Windows 2000, but you can still access the DOS window.

ONE MORE WAY TO CLEAR THE CACHE

There is one more way to clear your cache that is much easier. It involves going to the control panel. I will explain this way just to give you all the possible ways of doing this and because it is actually the easiest method. However, it is the most unreliable. Most of the time it will work fine, but there are rare cases when there is corruption in one of these directories, and this method might stop deleting at whatever corrupted file it comes across and it won't delete anything afterwards. That's why a lot of times, to make sure that all of the possible corruption is out of the cache, we would do the DOS Mode method. But for your information here it is:

Fig. 12 Internet Options in the control panel.

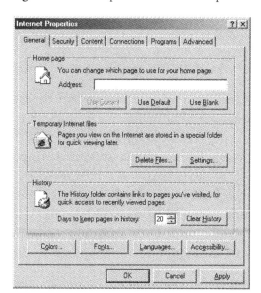

Click **Start** point to **Settings** then choose **Control Panel**. When control panel opens, you will see a bunch of icons in alphabetical order. Double-click on the one labeled **Internet**. It might say **Internet Options (fig. 12)** if you have Internet Explorer version 5.0 or above. Either way, double-click on it and click **Delete Files** under the Temporary Internet files heading. Click the check box that says either "Delete all offline content" or "Delete all subscription content" **(fig. 13)** and click **Ok**. When the mouse turns back into a pointer (or it's equivalent if you have a custom mouse cursor), you will know that it's done deleting the Temporary Internet Files. At the bottom of the same page click on where it says **Clear History** and click **Ok** to the message that comes up. When the mouse turns back into a pointer, it is done. You can just click **Ok** at the bottom and click the **X** in the upper-right corner to close Control Panel.

Fig. 13 You can delete content that you
          have saved to view offline.

CONTENT ADVISOR

During the course of your Web browsing, you may run across a Content Advisor error message. The Content Advisor is a parental control feature that you can configure in Microsoft Internet Explorer. If you get one of these messages, either the file that contains the Content Advisor information has become damaged or you or someone else has set one of these on the Web browser. Check Appendix I, *Content Advisor*, if you have any problems with this feature or any related error messages.

Web browser tips:

a) Favorites from IE to Netscape

To convert Favorites/Bookmarks back and forth between Internet Explorer and Netscape Navigator, pick up Microsoft's FavTool utility at http://www.microsoft.com/msdownload/ieplatform/favtool/favtool.asp.

b) Print Web page backgrounds

If you want to print a Web page the way it looks on your screen-with background color-you can enable background printing in Internet Explorer and Netscape Navigator. In IE , select Tools/Internet Options/Advanced. Scroll down to Printing and check the "Print background colors and images" box. Click on OK. In Navigator, select File/Page Setup, check Print Background under Page Options and click on OK. Remember: Printing the background will slow your print job and might obscure the text if you use a monochrome printer.

c) Print Web pages and include the time & date

You can set your browser to include time and date information when you print a Web page. Go to File/Page Setup in Navigator or IE. In Navigator, check "Date printed under footer," and your printouts will include the date and time. In IE, you can have the time and date printed in the header or footer. You have to enter the proper codes in the Header or Footer box. If you want the time and date, type &t &d in the appropriate text box. You might want to leave a few spaces between the codes to separate the time and date on the printed page.

d) Foreign Languages and the Web browser

Select View/Internet Options in Internet Explorer 4 or Tools/Internet Options in IE 5, open the General tab and click on the Languages button. Click on Add and then choose the language you want your browser to support from the list. You will find some resources below that will help if you are seeking support in Japanese or Chinese.

Japanese on your Web pages — http://www.shodouka.com

Japenese and Chinese software — http://www.twinbridge.com

Japenese tools and applications — http://www.pspinc.com

Chapter 9.5

Onward to the Internet

Now that you have read the primers and 9 chapters, you are ready to take the plunge into the deep divide we call the Internet. The Internet is a vast place where there are no definitive leaders and there are very few rules. You could think of it as the modern day old west. If you have an online service like America Online or CompuServe, you have access to the Internet plus you have the content that is specific to those online services and other perks that you can get only by being a member. These services are not "The Internet," however. In fact, no one entity is The Internet, but it is the culmination of what has become online services, ISPs, millions of Web sites, USENET and every other aspect of this vast universe.

Web sites are like pages of a book that can be viewed online, and in many cases a Web site will be quite a few pages. Thus a Web site can be a book in itself. Web sites are linked together in a matter of speaking because once you are online you can access any of them by typing in their Web address. In addition, these pages are joined together a lot of times with hyperlinks that will usually be displayed as a blue underlined word as illustrated in **fig. 14**. There are hyperlinks all over the Web. When you click on these links, it teleports you to a completely different Web site or sometimes it will take you to a different page on the same Web site. The name of the vast number of Web pages is so aptly named the World Wide Web.

Fig. 14 Example of hyperlinks on
aol.com. Notice all the blue
underlined words to the right.

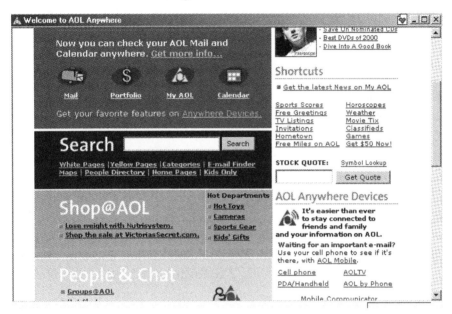

PICK A BROWSER ANY BROWSER

A browser is simply a program that reads Web pages on the Internet. The
two most popular browsers by far are Microsoft Internet Explorer and
Netscape Navigator although there are some more available, such as the
Opera Browser and Lynx. Browsers require *plug-ins* sometimes in order to
perform special functions. Plug-ins are little programs that enhance the
functionality of the browser in some way. For example, you might visit a
Web site that has sounds that you can hear, but first it will tell you that
you need to download a certain file so you can hear the sounds. This is a
plug-in because that little program plugs into your browser so you can

hear the sounds or see the videos that the Web site may have available. Plug-ins used to be called *helper applications.*

Fig. 15 Internet Explorer   **Fig. 16** Netscape

You can have many browsers on one computer, so some people might use Netscape as a rule but use Opera occasionally because of some feature that they like in that particular browser. It might even be the other way around: Someone will use Internet Explorer (**fig. 15**) or Netscape (**fig. 16**) once in a while, and they use another less popular browser most of the time. A browser is not a connection though, and therefore, you need to have an Internet provider or online service as your connection so that you can reach the Web and read Web pages with your Web browser.

ISN'T MY ISP THE INTERNET?

The main difference between an ISP (Internet service provider) and an online service is that an ISP will generally just provide a basic connection to the Internet and that's it. You dial up and there you are on the World Wide Web, and usually e-mail capability will be included in their package. One example of a good national-level ISP is Bellsouth.net. Online Services like America Online,

CompuServe, or Prodigy provide access to the Internet in addition to multiple e-mail addresses per account. They provide online content and features that are only available to members of these services, and they can often provide substantial savings on all kinds of products because of the large numbers of people that some of them deal with. These online services tend to be more user-friendly than plain-vanilla ISPs. You could think of the World Wide Web as a galaxy and in that galaxy, ISPs and Online services also exist. Of course, there are other galaxies where you would find other ISPs, online services, Web pages, Usenets, newsgroups, etc. The Internet would be the entire universe that is comprised of all of those galaxies.

Now you should be ready to surf the World Wide Web. You probably already have seen many URL addresses on TV or heard them on the radio unless you have been on Mars for the last 5 years. A URL is a *Universal Resource Locator*, and an example is www.microsoft.com. Simply put, a URL is a Web address. A quick review before we go on: HTML is *Hypertext Markup Language*, the programming language that Web pages are written in. HTTP is *Hypertext Transfer Protocol*, the protocol that is used to transfer Web pages to your computer via your browser. A URL is a **Universal Resource Locator** that is an actual Web address. Just like most people have a post office address, each Web site has a URL address. Now here's the kicker: Web sites also have a numeric address called an *IP address* (Internet Protocol address). These are usually in the format of something like 244.145.456.78. You can get to a Web site by typing in the numeric address such as http://244.145.456.78. Or, you could type in the URL address like www.pinkelephant.com. The Web site will actually come up faster if you know the numeric address.

When you type in a WWW address, computers called DNS servers translate the address into the numeric address. Servers are computers that move information along on the Internet. Some servers perform specific functions like a DNS (Domain Name Server) translates the URL into the numeric IP address so that your Web site can be found. Thus it stands to reason that if you can type in the numeric address, it will bypass the DNS server completely, thus saving a step (because you have already translated the address to the numeric IP address) and the page will come up faster.

So how do I find the numeric address you are thinking right? Well, these functions can be performed by a couple of different Windows commands called *ping* and *tracert*. A Trace Route is a bit more complex, and it will not only tell you what the IP address is, but it will actually tell you every server that the signal passes through from point A to point B. If you just want to find out the IP address, Ping will do just the same. Click on **Start** then **Run**. On the Run line type Ping {Whatever URL you want}. Say you want to find out the numeric IP address of the Disney Web site. Type in **ping www.disney.com** and click **Ok**. A Trace Route would work the same way. Type on the Run line **tracert www.disney.com** and click **Ok**.

Another way to find an IP address is to run WINIPCFG. The disadvantage of this command is that you actually have to be connected to the Web site first. You would make your connection to the Internet and click **Start>Run**. Type **winipcfg** on the Run line and click **Ok**. This will tell you the IP address as well as some other information such as the Subnet Mask.

Incidentally, you can get around most of your commercial parental control programs by just pinging the Web site that you want to get to and typing in the numeric IP address instead of the WWW address. The reason for this is that most of these programs look for keywords in the URL like porn, sex, etc. If you type in a number, obviously it won't have anything that the program will object to and it will let you through.

HOORAY FOR THE FREEBIES!

There are many freebies that can be had on the Internet these days; it seems as if companies vying for Web site "hits" are benefiting everyone. Well, it is benefiting anyone that is taking advantage of it anyway. There is so much competition on the Web these days that many companies are willing to break even or even lose money for the first several months or maybe even year that the company is in business in order to attract Web surfers. Their strategy optimistically hopes that attracting eyeballs will create return Web surfers, and whoever attracts the most eyeballs wins. Some of these dot com startups are doing whatever it takes to attract the largest number of surfers so that they can come up with a viable strategy to make money off of the whole deal in the future. Because of the new dot com business world, and millions and millions of dollars in venture capital that has been sunk into a lot of new dot coms, you as the consumer can benefit by getting free samples or free products. There are a lot of freebies where all you have to do is pay the shipping which is still a good deal. You might want to go to some freebie Web sites as soon as you start surfing the 'Net so you can get a new free mouse pad on the way while you are reading the rest of this book. You can go to any search engine and type in **freebies** for the search criteria. You will come up with plenty of options. I got a free mouse pad from www.freemousepads.com. Our freebies site is shown in **fig. 17**. Search engines are covered in *Compquest Volume 2, Chapter 20*, but some good ones to start out with are www.google.com, www.dogpile.com, www.lycos.com, and www.metacrawler.com. Or you can check out our search engines site illustrated in **fig. 18**.

Fig. 17 —our freebies site—www.compquest.org/freebies.htm

Fig. 18 —our search engines site—www.compquest.org/searchengines.htm

Also, check out **Appendix F**, *Our Take on All the Freebies*, for a subjective view about the subject.

Chapter #10

Software, Hardware, & Operating Systems:

Now that we are on Chapter 10 we are getting down to the nitty-gritty. You are still not ready yet to edit the Windows Registry, but you have come a long way by this time and I thought it was time for a challenging chapter like this. This chapter will elaborate on hardware, software, and we will talk a bit about operating systems if you didn't guess that from the title. You need to read and gain a full understanding of Chapter 11, *Manipulating Text*, because it explains how to copy & paste text. If copying & pasting text is just not making sense to you right now, don't worry because it will be explained at that time. After that, Chapter 13, *How to Move, Copy, Delete, and Rename files* and chapter 14, *How to Move, Copy, Delete, and Rename files part II*, outline some basic to intermediate functions that you can perform on your computer to move or copy files in the Windows environment. You will need to have the knowledge of the previous chapters, such as Chapter 12, *Files and the Directory Structure,* to understand those later chapters.

Before we talk about software, let me mention hardware one more time. Hardware in computer jargon is anything that is tangible. Were not just talking about all those cards, like your modem, that reside inside that mystery box, but your keyboard and mouse are hardware also because you can touch them right? Software is any program that you can execute on a computer. Basically, hardware is useless without software because software is the instructions that tell the hardware how to operate. This was the principle that Mr. Bill Gates, Microsoft's CEO, took advantage of more than 20 years ago. He had to convince IBM (aka Big Blue) that they needed his software or else all the high tech hardware that they had was little more than a junk heap. His software was an operating system known as DOS that evolved into Windows. Unfortunately for IBM they were a little near sighted at the time, and they didn't grab Mr. Gates up like they probably wish they would have. The IBM executives on the East Coast thought that what Mr. Gates was trying to sell them was something that they didn't really need. Actually, Bill Gates was far ahead of his time, and the rest of the world wasn't ready to accept the idea of an operating system for a computer. Bill ventured off on his own, Microsoft was born, and I hate to be cliché, but the rest is history.

Fig. 19 Computer hardware—shows an old Microsoft mouse, a modem, and a parallel port where you would usually hook up a printer.

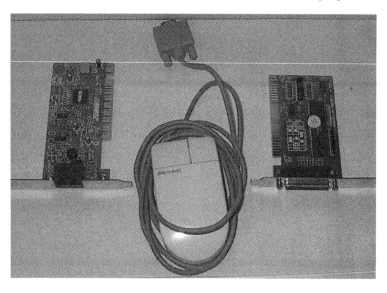

DOS IS FOR GEEKS

An operating system is something like Windows 95 or 98. Actually the first real operating system that would be widely used in the consumer market was DOS (Disk Operating System) that Bill Gates purchased for a mere $50,000. The guy who invented DOS is probably still kicking himself over that one. Notice that you don't hear too much about the guy that invented DOS, but look at how much Bill Gates is in the spotlight. Actually, the inventor of DOS created it while still in college. Rumor has it that Gates got the idea of what is called a GUI (Graphical User Interface) from Steve Jobs and the Apple Computer Company. To make a very long story short, this was how Windows and the Graphical User Interface for an IBM compatible computer was born.

A *Graphical User Interface* (GUI) was first presented with the Windows 3.x variety that preceded Windows 95. Windows 3.x simply laid on the top of DOS to give a little more user-friendliness to it. DOS is very prosaic and everything is done with command lines. There is nothing to click on and no pretty pictures, and as a result you pretty much have to be a computer geek to get things done in DOS. Windows 3.x, shown in **fig. 20**, was really not considered an Operating System, however. It was just a GUI that overlaid DOS. It wasn't until Windows 95, introduced in—you guessed it—1995, that a real Operating System evolved. Well, at least on the PC side. Some Macintosh aficionados would argue this point, but like I said, the first Operating System or OS for an IBM based machine.

Fig. 20 Win 3.x—shows the File Manager which is equivalent
to the Windows Explorer in later Windows versions.

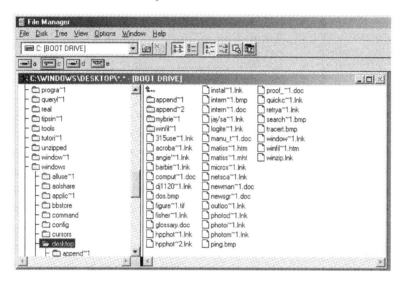

DOS was still under the skin of Windows 95, and to this day it remains as a subterranean dinosaur that hides under Windows. However, the principle of an OS is that it can really work independently of DOS. I will stop here before this gets a little too heavy, but the point is that a Graphical Interface is the pictures and graphics that appear in a modern Operating System. The Graphical User Interface (GUI) makes the OS much more user-friendly. The Operating System tells the computer how to function and the OS is software. Any program on a CD or a floppy disk that you can install on your computer is also software. There are little programs called drivers or device drivers that tell devices how to interact with Windows. For example, your modem has a device driver; without this driver installed it would not be able to function at all. Device drivers are also software because they can be installed, and they tell hardware how to act and interact with Windows.

Fig. 21 Hardware wizard

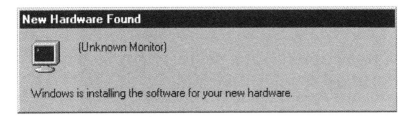

DEVICE DRIVERS

With the advent of Windows 98, there were many more drivers that came preinstalled even than on Windows 95. Because of this and because of *plug & play*, when you install hardware on your computer it may find the driver by itself without doing much of anything. **fig.** 21 illustrates how the Hardware Wizard in Windows will usually find newly installed hardware. However, most hardware like printers come with a disk, and during installation it may prompt you to put that disk in the CD-ROM drive in order to extract the driver from it. It is usually a good idea to use a disk that came with a piece of hardware even though it is quite possible that Windows will have a driver for it already on the system. The main reasons for using the driver disk is that the driver may be more up to date then the one already on the computer and it has the specific driver on it for a particular piece of hardware. For example, it may be specifically made for the Hewlett Packard DeskJet 1120C whereas the closest one in Windows 98 will be for the DeskJet 1120B. Although it may work, it would not be optimal for the printer and allow for it's best performance. That is strictly an example because I believe that Window 98 does contain a driver for that model of printer and I don't think HP made a DeskJet 1120B. However, Windows 95 would not have the driver for the DeskJet 1120C because the printer wasn't around yet at the time that Windows 95 hit the market place. Ideally, you should use the disk that comes with a particular device.

I HAVE A NEW COMPUTER SO WHY DO MY DEVICE DRIVERS NEED TO BE UPDATED?

Some things to note about device drivers and plug & play. Before Windows 95, hardware was referred to as *legacy* instead of *plug & play*. We had to manually configure hardware to work on a computer with Windows 3.1. This usually involved setting *jumpers* or *dip switches* on the actual piece of hardware itself. Hard drives are one of the only things around anymore that requires setting jumpers. Jumpering requires placing caps lined with metal over 2 little metal prongs on hardware to tell the computer exactly how to recognize it properly. Depending on how those caps are placed, a hard drive may be the master (main) drive or a slave (secondary) drive. Back in the legacy days, a modem might be configured for com 1 (communications port 1) or com 2 and that would be dependent on how the jumpers were placed. A lot of hardware back then had dip switches that worked on the same principles as jumpers but instead of placing metal-lined caps on pins there were perhaps 6 little switches that could be in the on or off position (up would be on and down would be off for instance and you could move them like a light switch). Hardware IRQs, I/O addresses, and com or serial ports were configured based on the placement of these switches. There is not much more you need to know about this except it usually was not a pleasant experience to say the least.

But those days are gone, and nowadays if you put hardware in the computer and turn on the machine, Windows will normally find the device—hence the name plug & play. An installation wizard will usually guide you through the process of setting it up, and you can be up and running in a matter of minutes with most hardware such as a modem or a sound card. One more thing that I should mention: The driver disk that comes with a device may not even be the latest driver for a particular piece of hardware. If you buy a brand new computer, there may already be an updated driver for one or more of the components such as the video card. This may seem strange, but it may have been six months to a year ago when they made that actual driver disk. In the meantime, the manufacturer of the computer or a particular piece of hardware may have made a new and improved driver, but they haven't burned it on a CD yet. You usually won't find out about this unless you have a compatibility problem such as your screen turns black after installing a certain program. In that example, you would need to seek an updated driver for your video card, most likely. You would want to contact the manufacturer of that card or the computer if the video card came with your computer. They would either send you the latest driver on a disk, or they might direct you to their Web site to download the driver in the event that it is so new that they haven't cut it on a disk yet.

Now that we know what software is and what the main software program on your computer is, which is the operating system, lets talk a little bit about how to move and copy files. First I want you to read and gain a full understanding of the next 2 chapters that are Chapter 11, *Manipulating Text* and Chapter 12, *Files and the Directory Structure*. Then we will pick up here on Chapter 13 *How to Move, Copy, Delete, and Rename Files*.

Chapter #11

Manipulating Text

The following is a neat trick that is worthy of an entire chapter. If you master this skill, you will save yourself countless hours over time on the computer. One trick that I do is if I am composing e-mail online, and I get far enough into it where if I suddenly got disconnected or my computer crashed and I lost my mail it would be devastating, I will send what I have so far to myself. Then I get the mail, keep it as new, (that way it stays on my ISP's mail server and it is not even on my computer) and copy and paste what I have so far in a new mail window. I continue typing, and if I lost my mail then, at least I would have up to the point when I last sent the mail to myself. This may seem either incomprehensible to you right now or maybe impossible. However, if you experiment after following the instructions below, you will probably understand exactly what I am talking about.

HOLD THE HEADERS PLEASE

Copying and pasting text is useful for many other situations: Let's say you get an e-mail that you want to print out, but you can't figure out how to get rid of those pesky mail headers. Headers are those cryptic addresses that show who the e-mail was sent from and who it was sent to and everywhere in between. There is a simple solution to this. Just copy only the body of the letter, or what you want to print, and paste it in a new mail window and print it out from there. By the way, I usually compose mail offline and choose to send it later. That way if I get disconnected, I don't lose my mail. The next time I happen to connect, my ISP will ask me if I want to send my mail, and I say Yes.

It is amazing how many really irate people I have talked to that lost a 1000 word letter simply because they weren't aware of these 2 principles. For your information, the keyboard command to copy text is **CTRL+C** and to paste it in another document it is **CTRL+V**. The keyboard command to cut text is **CTRL+X**. You want to cut instead of copy if you don't want the text to remain in the original document. I rarely cut text because when you copy it leaves the original text behind that serves as a backup. In addition, the undo keyboard command is **CTRL+Z**. Undo can be used in most programs to undo your last action. So if you make a blunder, try pressing **CTRL+Z** and see if it voids your mistake. Some programs support multiple undos, and some will only go back one move even if you press **CTRL+Z** over and over. See Appendix B at the end of this book for some more keyboard commands.

How to copy & paste text:

Text can be easily transferred from one document to another with the Copy and Paste functions available from the Edit menu. You can copy text from online areas that may be available on your Internet Provider (chat, e-mail, Instant Message notes, and member profiles) and paste the sections into e-mail, text files, or input boxes. You can copy and paste from almost any program in Windows to any other program. The only reason it wouldn't work, would be a situation where you are pasting a graphics file in a program that can only handle text files or something along those lines.

Fig. 22   Drag the mouse from upper-left to lower-right in a diagonal fashion to select (highlight) text.
Click Copy from the Edit menu.

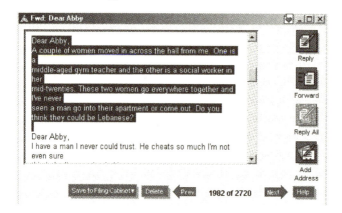

Fig. 23 Click inside a new mail window or wherever you want
to put the text and click Paste from the Edit menu.

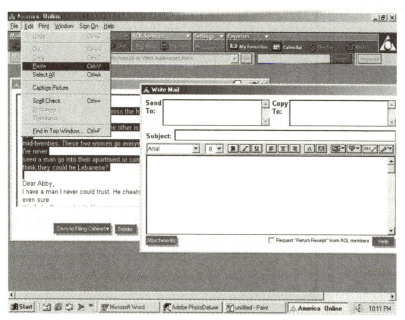

1. Hold down the mouse button and drag the mouse over the text to highlight the information you want to copy.

2. Let go of the mouse button.

3. Select **Copy** from the Edit menu. A copy of the text is held in your computer's memory.

4. Place the cursor in the space where you want to paste and click once.
5. Select **Paste** from the Edit menu. The text appears in the new space.

Fig. 24 Shows text that appears in the new space.

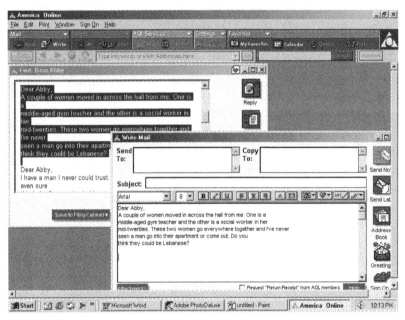

How to copy & paste in Paint:

The following will illustrate how to make a copy of what is on your computer screen even if, or I should say especially if, it is graphical in nature. You see the Paint program is something that can be accessed from the Accessories menu (**Start>Programs>Accessories**), and it is usually automatically installed in Windows. If it isn't on your computer, it can be added in Add/Remove programs in the Control panel provided that you have your Windows CD. You can also click your **Start** button then **Run**. On the Run line where it says Open, type **mspaint** then click **Ok**. It doesn't matter whether you use capital letters or not, and you can use a mixture of small letters and caps because it is not case sensitive. I will use caps in this book sometimes to emphasize certain things, but very few things in Windows are case sensitive. Paint can view *bitmap* images that are rather large but detailed graphics files. Bring your screen up so that you are looking at the part that you want to copy into Paint or print out. This could be your Windows Desktop, Windows Explorer or any screenshot that you may want to use. Press the **ALT+PRINT SCREEN** keys on your keyboard. The Print Screen key is in the upper right corner of the keyboard next to the **F12** key. The **ALT** key is in the lower-left portion of your keyboard next to the spacebar. After that, minimize whatever program you are in, if any, by clicking the minus sign in the upper-right corner of your screen.

Fig. 25 Edit>Paste in Paint.

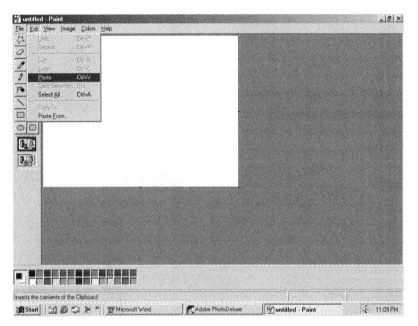

Go to Paint, by clicking on **Start >Programs>Accessories>Paint**. Click on **Edit** over the toolbar and click on **Paste**. You will be looking at a window similar to that shown in **fig. 25**. It will put the most active window you can see on your screen in here; if you press just the **Print Screen** button and not **ALT+Print Screen**, it will copy everything shown on your entire monitor screen and not just the window that's in the foreground. You can click **File** then **Print** at the top if you want to print the screenshot. Or, if you want to save the file, you can click **File** then **Save As** as shown in **fig. 26**. Type a file name and make sure that you select the correct destination at the top. For example, if you want to save the file on a floppy disk, choose 3 ½ floppy (A:), and if you want to save the file on your Desktop, choose Desktop. It's up to you, but I like to save things to the Desktop and then move or copy them from there. The reason why I do this a lot is because I can easily view the file if I minimize Paint.

Fig. 26 File>Save As… in Paint.

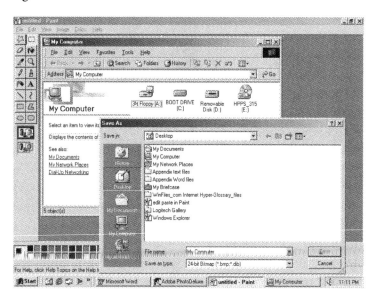

Don't forget that you may have minimized the program you are in to paste your screenshot into the Paint program. If you did minimize a program or window before opening Paint, you can click on the program name at the bottom (on the Taskbar show in **fig. 28**) to bring it back up to a full screen. The *Taskbar* is the portion usually at the bottom of your Windows Desktop that is between the Start button and the *Systray* (System Tray), where you will usually find a clock and maybe a little megaphone that lets you control the speaker volume. And yes that is the principle we used to put screenshots into this book such as the Windows Explorer screen shown in Paint in **fig. 27**.

Fig. 27 Explorer window in MsPaint.

However, like I said, the Paint program saves a file as a bitmap image (extension .bmp), and the file is usually going to be rather large. This would take too much time to upload and download if you wanted to attach a file and send it to someone via e-mail. Therefore, unless you want your friends to get mad at you for sending a file that will take them an hour to download, it may be necessary to convert the Bitmap into a smaller file format such as a GIF (Pronounced jiff—extension .gif). You may be able to save your file as a different file format in your scanner or camera software. If not, the conversion can be done with any decent graphics editing program such as PaintShop Pro, Adobe PhotoShop, or I use Adobe Photo Deluxe lately for these purposes.

Fig. 28 Taskbar with Systray (System tray) shown to the right and the Start button to the left.

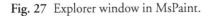

Chapter #12

Files & the Directory Structure

THE VIRTUAL FILING CABINET

A computer's hard drive holds all of the computer's information. The information on a computer is organized into files much like papers would be organized into files in a metal filing cabinet. Except of course being a computer it does differ slightly from a tangible filing cabinet. First of all, as you may already know, all the drives on a computer have a letter assigned to them. The floppy drive is usually labeled A, the hard drive C, the CD-ROM drive is normally drive D; if you have any other drives than these 3, things may change a bit with the lettering. Also, don't confuse this with the lettering of A-Z that is associated with a traditional filing cabinet where you might have 3 drawers. The first one A-G, the second one H-P, and the third drawer would house Q-Z.

You can have more than 1 hard drive. If you have 2 drives, the 1st hard drive is labeled C, the 2nd one D, and the CD-ROM drive would be pushed up to letter E. The CD-ROM drive might be another letter in that example such as G. You can also have a partitioned hard drive in lieu of having 2 separate physical hard drives. A *partition* is really just like a wall that separates one hard drive into at least 2 sections. Picture a room with a wall constructed right down the center of it. One half of the room we could call C and the other half D. See **fig. 29**.

Fig. 29 Partitions shown where the C and D drives
are divided into equal parts.

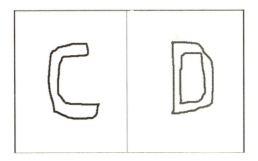

In real life construction, and with a computer drive, you can place that "wall" or partition anywhere. So in a room, the C part might be 90% of the room and the D part the other 10% or however you wanted to do it. See **fig. 30.**

Fig. 30 Partitions shown where the C drive
can hold 90% of the information
and the D drive holds the other 10%.

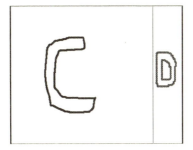

BE SURE TO BACK UP YOUR FILES

There is really no limit to the number of partitions that you can set up, that I am aware of, but you can reach a point of diminishing efficiency. Think of a 10' x 10' room that has 9 partitions so that it cuts the room into 10 small sections that are 1 foot wide and 8 feet high (See **fig. 31**). The room wouldn't exactly be useful would it? You may ask well, "why would you partition a drive at all?" The answer is you shouldn't attempt it unless you know what you are doing. There is a program that's built into Windows called *fdisk* that will enable you to partition a drive, but you will lose all your information on that drive and Windows will even need to be reinstalled. There are programs that are very good at partitioning drives, and under normal circumstances, you will not even lose any of your information. One of these programs is PowerQuest's Partition Magic. Although Partition Magic will usually allow you to partition your drive without losing any information or files, there is always a chance that your hard drive will crash when making any system-level changes on your computer—or even when you don't make any changes and you least expect it. PowerQuest's program, as well as other similar utilities, have disclaimers to that effect. Bottom line: **Always have your important files backed up no matter what!**

Fig. 31 Drive Partitioned in 10 sections

Like the old adage goes, don't put all your eggs in one basket. The same holds true even in the computer age. So the next time you get a chance, and certainly before making any major changes to your computer, I would recommend backing up anything important. Think about what would happen if you lost all of the files on your computer right now. If it would mean a lot to you, then back your system up. If you don't know how, contact your computer manufacturer and ask them. Or, click on **Start>Programs>Accessories>System Tools>Backup** and follow the onscreen instructions. Click **Help** and choose **Help Topics** at the top for more detailed information on using this utility.

TIP Use Xcopy to copy files from one drive to another:

Xcopy is a Dos command that is useful to copy files from one drive to another. Sometimes, you won't be able to get all files from a drive to copy to another drive while in

Windows. This is especially true if you are trying to copy your C drive and some of the files are going to tell you that they are in use because your Windows files will be installed on drive C. and Windows will be running. Not only is this information useful for backups, but it is a quick and easy way to copy the entire contents of a drive to another drive. If you get a larger hard drive and install it, it is likely that your original drive where Windows is installed will become the D drive and your new larger hard drive will be drive C. You can use xcopy to conveniently copy everything from drive D to C, which not only will retain your files on the main drive but you won't even need to reinstall Windows in most cases. You could then turn around and format the D drive and start out with a clean drive that would be your secondary drive at that point. To find out the available switches (options) for any Dos command, type the command followed by a space, forward slash and a question mark (xcopy /?).

If you want to copy the entire contents of one drive to another, you use the format as shown below. Just get to a C prompt (C:\>) and type the following command that you may need to alter a little to fit your situation. The command below will copy the entire contents of the C drive and copy then to the D drive.

xcopy c:*.* /e/h/k/r/c d:

Okay, now that I have gone off on my little tangent let's get back to the question. We have established that unless you know what you're doing you will probably end up doing more harm than good by partitioning your hard drive. The only time that it is really beneficial to do this from a performance point of view is if you have a very large hard drive. Because of the way the hard drive structure works, it actually enables a hard drive to hold more information if you break it down into smaller sections. Most large drives these days come with a user-friendly disk utility that offers you the option of partitioning your drive. From a practical point of view, partitioning a drive may help with the organization of your files: You may want to put all of your personal files on a 2nd partition and only have your Windows System files on drive C. If you don't want to get to technical, that's about all that you need to know about partitioning drives.

Fig. 32 Hierarchical file order showing a glimpse of the Windows Explorer
and how the root directories fall directly beneath the C drive.

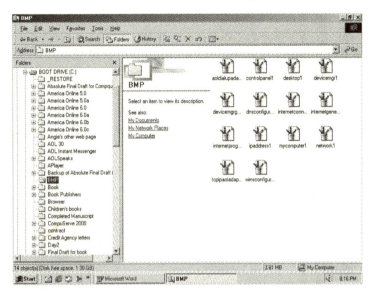

One thing that will always remain a constant on a Windows machine
amidst all the possible configurations is that the main drive where
Windows is installed is going to be drive C. A directory installed directly
on the C drive is commonly called a ***root directory***. This term just means
that a directory isn't a subdirectory or isn't a file inside of a directory, but it
is installed at the top of the hierarchical order on the C drive. Notice how
in **fig. 32**, the C drive is at the top of the structure; root directories fall
beneath that. Inside of those root directories, there will often be subdirectories. A root directory is just a main directory that is directly on the C
drive (or another drive).

If we compared this to a traditional filing cabinet again, the entire cabinet would be your entire hard drive, and a drawer in the filing cabinet would be the C drive or partition. If you just had one big C drive and no partitions, it would be like having one big filing cabinet with no separate drawers. Although you can't compare everything equally between a computer and a tangible filing cabinet: It is fine to have one big hard drive with no other partitions, but a standard filing cabinet, that usually has 3 drawers, would be kind of silly if we made it with 1 drawer that would be about 4 feet deep. The drawer may contain separators that would separate the manila folders in some way. These separators would be the main or root directories on a computer. In other words, a directory is the highest level file on a drive. Inside the drawer we usually have manila folders in alphabetical order right? These folders would separate the different documents into some semblance of order. These are called folders on a computer as well. Not coincidentally, these folders will look like little manila folders on your computer. Inside the folders in the metal filing cabinet, there will be papers of some sort commonly called files. Contents of folders on a computer are also called files.

To recap this from largest to smallest: **Drive**, **Partition** (may just have 1 partition or C drive), **Directory**, **Folder**, and **File**. So that there is some order to all of this, and so that you and the computer can find what file you or it needs, there are paths to every file, folder or directory on a computer. Read on and we will discuss this in further detail.

Fig. 33 Windows directory shown. Notice how the System directory
Resides in Windows and therefore is a subdirectory of the
Windows directory.

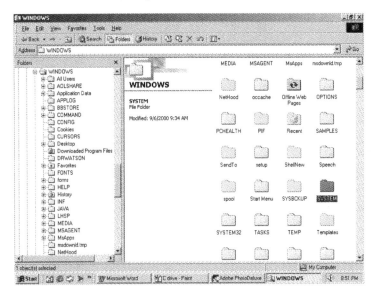

CUT A PATH TO YOUR NEAREST DIRECTORY

A directory that will definitely be on the C drive is the Windows directory
(see **fig. 33**).

This is where the Windows program is actually installed and all of the crucial operating system files are in this directory or in the System directory.
The System directory resides in the Windows directory. Therefore, System
is a subdirectory of the Windows directory. You can have a maximum of
512 root directories in Windows 95/98. Windows will tell you that it cannot create a directory if you try to make one and are already at the maximum. You can always make subdirectories within these root directories
though; the number of subdirectories is only limited by the amount of
drive space.

There are paths on a computer that tell you and the computer where to find files. A ***directory path*** to a file might be something like **C:\Windows\System**. Lets say that we have a folder named Vmm32 in the **Windows\System** directory to give you a realistic example because Vmm32 is a folder that you will usually find. Inside the Vmm32 folder lets say there is a file called Run to give you an unrealistic example because there probably won't be a file called Run in there. What would the path be to the file called Run? It would be: **C:\Windows\System\Vmm32\Run**. Do you get it? The computer knows that it can find the file called Run on the C drive in the Windows directory in the System directory (You can have directories inside of directories) and inside of the folder called Vmm32. You can tell programs to run by typing them on the run line (you get there by clicking **Start>Run**). That's why a lot of programs will tell you to insert the CD-ROM and type in D:\setup. There is a file called **setup** on the root directory of the CD-ROM when instructions that accompany a CD tell you to type D:\setup. You can run any program on your hard drive by typing a command line if you know the path to it.

GET A BIRDS-EYE VIEW OF YOUR FILES

There is something called the Windows Explorer that is intended primarily to give you a glimpse of all the files on the computer. The path to Windows Explorer is **Start>Programs>Windows Explorer**. Get a glimpse of the Windows Explorer by looking at **fig. 32** and **33**. That kind of path is different from a directory path. One type of path that is shown in this book a lot tells you what to click on and in what order to get somewhere on your computer; the symbol (**>**) is shorthand and just means "then." Such as click Start **then** Programs **then** Windows Explorer. A directory path tells you exactly where a certain file is located on the computer. Incidentally, there are some command words that you can type on the run line that Windows will recognize. For example, you can just type **explorer** on the run line and click **Ok**; this will bring up the Windows Explorer.

You can type in **control** and bring up the control panel or type in **command** and bring up a DOS window. In such cases, it is not necessary to type out the entire directory path to run a particular program rather just the single words.

Back to the Windows Explorer. Notice that the main or root directories have a plus sign (+) next to them. If you look up at the top, you will see something called My Computer. If this has a minus sign (-) next to it, click inside the little square where the minus sign is and it should fold everything up and make the sign next to My Computer a plus (+). After experimenting with this for a minute or two, you can conclude that these signs expand or collapse the directories to bring them in or out of your view.

Lets start there where there is a plus sign (+) next to My Computer because all the directories will be collapsed. Click on the Plus sign next to My Computer and it will drop down all of your drives as shown in **fig. 34**. If there are any minus signs under My Computer, click on those to turn them into pluses, and you should now see only the drives on the computer and none of the files or directories on those drives. Now find the C drive and click on the Plus next to it, and you will be looking at all of the main (root) directories again on your main drive that we previously established as being your C drive. The reason why all of them may not have a plus sign is because there may be a directory inside of a directory. The subdirectory will not have a plus sign next to it. Another reason why a directory may not have a sign next to it is because it is empty. The only reason for a plus sign is if there is something to expand, and if the directory is empty, there won't be.

Right-click menu in Windows Explorer

TIP Normally, when you right-click a file in Windows Explorer, a
Context menu appears with options to open, view, cut, copy,
rename files and so forth. But if you hold the Shift key while

you right-click a file, you'll see an entirely different Context menu. The Shift right-click menu allows you to alter the file view (so you can see small or large icons, details, and so on), rearrange the icons, or create a new folder or file. Or, you can choose the Open With… option to open a file with a specified application.

Fig. 34 Expanded drive view in Windows Explorer.

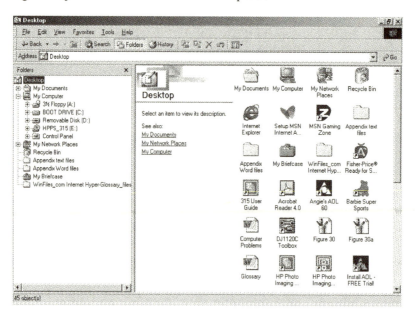

PUTTING IT ALL TOGETHER NOW

Now that you should have a feel for the directory structure in Windows, lets look at one of the practical uses of this knowledge. Sometimes you might have a CD, and it will not start to run automatically. If instructions came with it, they might tell you to click on **Start>Run** and type in D:\setup where D=your CD-ROM drive letter. Occasionally this will not work, and you will need to explore or browse the disk in order to find the setup file. First I must explain that a CD-ROM, or any kind of disk for that matter, like a 3 ½ floppy, has the same basic directory structure as the hard drive on your computer. Don't get this confused with the structure of the drive itself, but there will be directories, folders, and files in a hierarchical order. Also, a CD-ROM might have more than one partition. There might be one partition that has the setup files for a Macintosh that is not viewable on a PC, and likewise the PC files would not be visible on a Macintosh computer. That would be the case where a program is supported on both a PC and a MAC of course. We will take a look at the directory structure of the America Online version 6.0 compact disk. I decided to use this as an example because of the ubiquity of the AOL disk; a lot of people have one of them around the house whether they are an AOL member or not and you can usually find one in many retail outlets. Many people may put this book to good use and sign up for AOL, and it provides a good example of a directory structure because there is quite a bit more than meets the eye on this CD. Incidentally, it has a Macintosh partition, but of course we won't see it since we are working with PCs.

To get to this directory structure view, you can go a few different paths. One of them is to open up My Computer (Double-click the My Computer icon on your Desktop). Right-click once on the CD-ROM drive icon. The right mouse button will produce a drop-down menu that is only viewable from…well…right-clicking. From the right-click drop-down menu, left-click once on **Explore**. This brings up a Windows Explorer type view of the drive. Look underneath the CD-ROM drive, and you may see all of the root directories (see **fig. 35**). You may need to click the plus (+) sign next to the CD-ROM if you don't see any directories, and that will turn the sign next to the drive into a minus (-) and thus show you all of the directories.

Fig. 35 Explore CD Window. You get to this by right-clicking on the CD-ROM drive icon and left-clicking on Explore.

Fig. 36 Browse window from Find Files or Folders

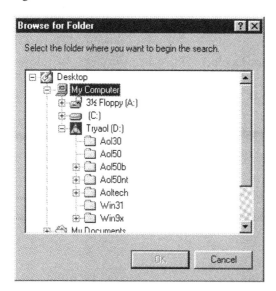

Another option is to click on **Start>Find>Files or Folders**. Click on the **Browse** button and then click on the plus (+) next to the CD-ROM drive as shown in **fig. 36**. Incidentally, Windows by default will show you whatever the name of the CD is and then the letter of the drive. In this case the name of the CD is Tryaol and the CD-ROM drive is letter D. That's why it says Tryaol (D:). From here you will get essentially the same screen as you had when you explored the CD in My Computer. If you wanted to install AOL 6.0, you would just click on the AOL icon that is to the left of Tryaol (D:) because the setup file for AOL version 6.0 is a root directory on the CD. Then click **Ok** at the bottom that should be lit up at that point. Click on **Find Now** to the right. This will search for and show you all of the root directories. From there just scroll down until you see the AOL icon in front of where it says Setup and double-click on **Setup** or the AOL icon next to it to kick off the installation.

Sometimes, you may not see all of the directories that I am describing or that you see in the illustrations. The most likely reason for this is because the computer is configured not to show hidden files. All you have to do is open up My Computer. Click **View>Options** in Windows 95, **View>Folder Options** in Windows 98, and **Tools>Folder Options** in Windows Me. Click inside the little circle where it says **Show hidden files and folders** (the wording may vary depending on your version of Windows, but basically you want to show all files).

If you had Windows 3.1, you would want to scroll down until you reached the Win31 folder. This is a directory so it will appear as a manila folder and it will have contents in it. Double-click on the manila folder and there will be a setup file called Setup16. Just double-click on **Setup16**, and it will install AOL 4.0 for Windows 3.1. You could install this one on Windows 95 or Windows 98 if you have an older computer or you are low on drive space. This would install the AOL 4.0 version for Windows 3.1 that doesn't require as much memory or drive space as the AOL 4.0 for Windows 95 and 98.

If you wanted to install just Microsoft Internet Explorer 5.0 that's no problem. When you are looking at the list of folders after clicking on **Find Now**, look for and double-click on the Manila Folder labeled **AOL50B**. Double-click on **MSIE5.0**. And there's your setup file **IE50**. All you have to do to kick off the installation of the Explorer Web browser is to double-click on **IE50**. If you want to install Internet Explorer 5.5, double-click on the **AOLTECH** folder then open up the **WINDOWSME BROWSER** folder. The setup file is **MSIE55**. Just double-click on that folder to start the installation.

Windows Me changed the whole look and feel of the Find Files utility. You get there by clicking on **Start>Search>For Files or Folders...** You really can't browse the CD-ROM like you could in previous Windows versions here, but you could search for *.exe to bring up all the executable files on the CD. See **fig. 37** for the Windows Me search results for the executable files from the AOL60 CD. Just make sure where it says **Look in:** you choose the CD-ROM drive from the drop-down menu in a case like this since that is the drive you are looking in. It is labeled TRYAOL (E:) in this example, also shown in fig. 37.

One more way that you can access the contents of a CD is from the Windows Explorer. You can access all of the files of your hard drive from Window Explorer, so it just makes sense that you can access all of the files of any drive right? Click **Start>Programs>Windows Explorer**. On Windows Me, click **Start>Run**. On the Run line type **explorer** and click **Ok**. Look in the upper-left portion of this screen and from there it is really the same thing that you get when you right-click on the CD-ROM icon and left-click on **Explore** in the My Computer Window (see **fig. 35**). Again to run the AOL 6.0 setup, expand My Computer by clicking the + sign to the left of it. Double-click on the CD-ROM drive icon (TRYAOL and the letter of your CD-ROM drive) and then click on **Setup** located in the right-hand window. You see the Windows Explorer is a 2-pane view; if you click on a directory on the left-hand side, it will show you all the contents of the directory on the right-hand side.

Fig. 37 Windows Me Search for Files or Folders...

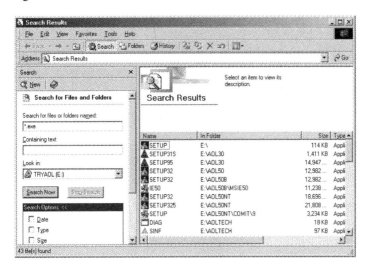

Actually, the preferable way to do this (and probably the easiest) is from the Windows Explorer. This doesn't involve any right clicking, and it is pretty straightforward.

The AOL 4.0 directory structure is outlined below to illustrate one type of directory view:

AOL 4.0 CD contents

Aol30
|__ Setup31.exe 4,471 kb 7/14/97
|__ Setup95.exe 14,947 kb 3/4/98

Win31
|__ Setup16.exe 6,677 kb 9/19/98
|___Addons
| |_____Goodie16.exe
| |
| |_____Realpl5
| | |__ Real_pla.txt
| | |__ Realplay.exe
| | |__ Realplay.ico
| |
| |_____Shokwav

| |__Direct.exe
| |__Macromed.txt

| |__Sw4bit.ico
|___Art
|__Art5.idx

Win9x
|__Setup32.exe 9,605 kb 9/19/98
|
|__Addons
| |__Goodie32.exe

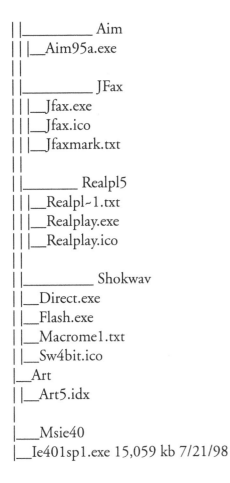

```
| |_____ Aim
| | |__Aim95a.exe
| |
| |_____ JFax
| | |__Jfax.exe
| | |__Jfax.ico
| | |__Jfaxmark.txt
| |
| |_____ Realpl5
| | |__Realpl~1.txt
| | |__Realplay.exe
| | |__Realplay.ico
| |
| |_____ Shokwav
| |__Direct.exe
| |__Flash.exe
| |__Macrome1.txt
| |__Sw4bit.ico
|__Art
| |__Art5.idx
|
|___Msie40
|__Ie401sp1.exe 15,059 kb 7/21/98
```

Hopefully, now you have a decent understanding of the directory structure on your computer and on drives in general. It is really pretty simple once you see how it's done. Don't let the fact that it is a computer freak you out and make your mind go blank. That's why I made an analogy to a traditional filing cabinet; they really work the same way in this respect. If you are thoroughly confused about this chapter, don't worry about it right now. Go on to chapter 13 *How to Move, Copy, Delete, and Rename files.* Come back to this one if you want to later on. You might grasp it better after going through the rest of the book. This is one of those chapters that will probably make no sense unless you step through it on a computer while you are reading it. If you do, I think that it will be fairly easy. If you want to learn about drive structures, read *4Windows File Systems What you need to know about Fat 16, Fat 32, and NTFS* noted in Appendix H, *Resources.*

So far in this chapter, we have looked at the way files are arranged on a drive. Drive structures are actually the way drives are constructed to hold these files. It's hard to make an analogy to our filing cabinet with drive structures. I suppose this would look at where the welds are placed to hold the cabinet together, and how there are those metal tracks so that the drawers can slide in and out, and how the drawers have those little plastic wheels to make the drawers slide easier.

Fig. 38 AOL60 CD view.

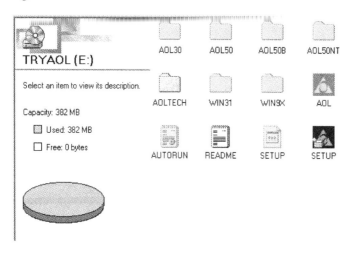

AOL 6.0 Directory Structure

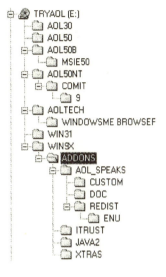

Chapter #13

How to Move, Copy, Delete, and Rename files

As an introduction to this chapter, I feel obligated to explain what you will probably see on your computer, why these things are there, and what they do. In the last chapter we looked at how files are structured on the Windows platform. Don't worry I won't talk about the difference between FAT16 and FAT32 disk partitions or clusters and sectors on a hard disk. I will explain what you see on your computer, what the icons mean and the functions that these things perform.

Let's start on the Windows Desktop since you will spend most of your time there when you are not online. The Desktop is the screen that comes up when you first turn your computer on. It is pictured in **fig 39**. The Desktop usually has a **Start** button in the lower-left hand corner (it can be located in the upper-left or somewhere else) if you have not moved it elsewhere.

TIP Put your Desktop icons to the right:

Ever wish your desktop icons were lined up on the right side of the desktop? Try this. Right-click the desktop, select Arrange Icons and be sure Auto Arrange is turned off. Highlight all your desktop icons, then drag and drop them to the right side. Now just right-click the Desktop and choose Line Up Icons to straighten them out.

Fig. 39 Windows Desktop.

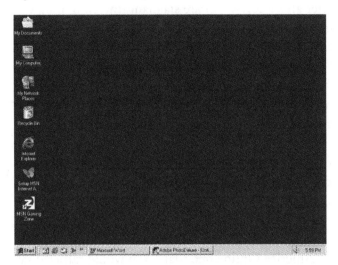

THE ICONS ARE ONLY SHORTCUTS

Other things that characterize the Desktop are the My Computer icon and the Recycle Bin. There are many other icons that might be on the Desktop. Icons by the way are the little pictures that you can click on to open a program. You may see an icon for Internet Explorer, My Documents, My briefcase, and any other icon that represents the programs that you have installed on your computer.

When you install a program it will put an icon on your Desktop. It may also enter its name on the Programs menu. You can launch the program by clicking on **Start** then up to **Programs** then find the program's listing on the cascading menu to the right and click on it. Also, you can launch the program by clicking on the icon on the Desktop. Some programs give you the option during the installation to create a Desktop icon or not or to create a listing on the Programs menu or not. Most of the icons are expendable meaning that you could delete them with no consequences. However, My Computer and Recycle bin are stagnant, meaning they will be there and you cannot get rid of them. Actually you can get rid of them by editing the Windows Registry, a program that controls the most rudimentary functions of Windows. You do **not** want to get rid of them anyway though or else Windows may fail to function like it is supposed to. Also, you do not want to edit the Registry because any little mistake that you make in there can turn your computer into a $1000 toaster.

Understand that all of these things on the Desktop are merely shortcuts that point to the real programs that are located on your hard disk. Shortcuts are denoted by a little curved arrow in the lower-left corner of the icon. See the shortcuts illustrated in **fig. 40**. There are 7 shortcut icons next to each other horizontally. Let's say that you have America Online and the icon is labeled "America Online free trial." You would rather it say "My AOL." No problem. You can name the icon anything you want. Remember that it is just a shortcut. Here's how to rename an icon:

Fig. 40 Shortcut icons.

TIP Start Menu tips:

When you add a listing to your Start menu by dragging and dropping it onto the Start button, you're really just adding a shortcut to the folder. It's usually better to put the actual folder there instead of a shortcut. The Start menu is just a special folder in the Windows folder called, Start Menu, which may not come as much of a surprise. If you put folders that contain your documents into this folder, you gain several advantages. What you see on the Start menu is always current. If you delete a folder, it disappears from the Start menu as well while a shortcut would remain, for instance. Also, actual folders appear on the Start menu as cascading menu items, whereas shortcuts to folders just open the folder on your Desktop when selected. In addition, the Start menu is always accessible, even if your Desktop is cluttered or you are in another program that is covering the Desktop.

File renaming instructions:

Right-click your mouse on the icon (or file) that you want to rename. A drop-down menu will appear. Refer to **fig. 41** and **fig. 42** that illustrate renaming an icon. Left-click on **Rename**. You will notice that it will high-light the current name of the file. Hit the **DELETE** key on the right-hand side of your keyboard (included in the 6 keys that include INSERT, HOME, PAGE UP, PAGE DOWN, END, AND DELETE next to the number pad at the far right side of your keyboard). This will erase the old name. Now type in what you want for a name—be creative! When you are done typing the name that you want, hit the **Enter** key on your keyboard to confirm your choice. Pretty neat huh? Just remember not to get too cocky renaming files. You can rename any icon on the Desktop that will let you rename it without causing a problem. But, you can really mess things up if you start arbitrarily renaming all kinds of files on your system. Have fun but, like I said before, don't make me say I told you so!

Fig. 41 Right-click drop-down menu.

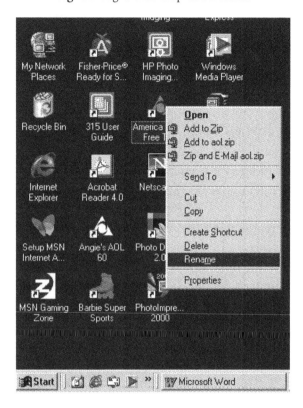

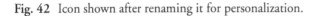

Fig. 42 Icon shown after renaming it for personalization.

ARE YOU READY TO GET A LITTLE IN-DEPTH ON THIS?

Let's say that you delete an icon and you want to get it back. You can create a shortcut to any file on your computer. What you need to do is draw a shortcut to the executable file within a program. An executable file can be recognized by the 3-letter extension .exe. Let's continue to use AOL as an example: The executable file for AOL is AOL.EXE. You can usually recognize the executable also because it will have a tiny icon that looks just like the one on the Desktop, but it is much smaller. This tiny picture of an icon is sometimes called a *thumbnail*. To get a glimpse of this, let's navigate to the Windows Explorer. Click on **Start>Programs>Windows Explorer**. This will take you to a screen that has a bunch of files on the left-hand side. If you have AOL, double-click on the America Online folder on the left-hand side. It may say America Online 5.0 or 6.0 or something similar. The contents of the America Online folder will then be on the right-hand side. Look for the one with the AOL icon. The name next to the icon will probably only say AOL and not AOL.EXE because sometimes your computer is configured not to show file extensions. If you do not have AOL, try this with another program like your ISP so you can follow along. CompuServe 2000 will work in a similar manner, for instance.

Double-click on the AOL icon, and it should launch the program just as if you had clicked on the Desktop icon. If you are "mouse challenged," right-click on the AOL icon and left-click on **Open**. Pretty freaky again isn't it?

Make a note of the name of the executable file that you found. Go ahead and close the Explorer by clicking the **X** in the upper-right corner. Now we are going to make an icon. If you have AOL go ahead and delete your current Desktop AOL icon. If not, make sure you know the name of your other executable file that you found. If you have CompuServe 2000, it would be CS.EXE. If you found an executable file in the Windows Explorer that is also on the Desktop, Delete the icon on your Desktop by right-clicking it, and then click on **Delete** and say **Yes** to send that baby to the recycle bin. Go ahead be brave. You can always restore the icon out of the recycle bin. Is the icon gone now? Good—now on to the next chapter....just kidding ;-P

How to create a Desktop icon:

Click on **Start** then point to **Find** and choose **Files or Folders** to your right. If you have Windows Me, it will be **Start** then **Search>For Files or Folders**.... In the box labeled Named, or Search for Files or Folders Named in Windows Me, type in aol.exe or whatever the executable file name was that you noted in the previous step. Where it says Look in we want to make it look in the C drive or My Computer. The latter will make the search encompass all drives on the computer. To change the Look in, just click the little down arrow (s) on the right side of the **Look In** line. A window will drop down with everything that you can select. This is called a *drop-down menu*. Select either My Computer or C drive. C drive may look like (C:), or HP Pavilion C, or something (C:). Once you have that selected, click **Find Now** on the right-hand side. Or click **Search Now** at the bottom left on Windows Me.

You will see the magnifying glass move around in a circle, and it will finally come up with your search results. You will probably only see one thing that it found at the bottom of this screen, but in the case of AOL, you might see one that says it is located in C:\Americaonline 5.0 and another that says C:\Americaonline 5.0a. You might even see several or more, but if this is the case, we want to concentrate on the one with the highest letter in the alphabet. In other words, if there are AOLa, AOLb, AOLc, and AOLd, we will be working with AOLd. If it only finds one file, then obviously we will be working with that one. It will tell you over to the right of where it found the file where it is located on the computer. This is called the path of the file as discussed in Chapter 12. The path will be under the heading In Folder. Furthermore, at the bottom left-hand corner it will tell you how many files of this name that the search found on your computer, for example, 4 file(s) found.

Now that we have established which one we will be creating a shortcut to, look to the left of where it found the file aol.exe that may only say AOL. You will see that tiny AOL icon again. If you have another executable file besides aol.exe, just use the same principle and right-click on the little icon to the left of the file name. After right-clicking on the little icon to the left, left-click on **Create Shortcut Here**. You will get a subsequent message: "A shortcut cannot be created here. Would you like the shortcut to be created on the Desktop instead?" as shown in **fig. 43**. Say **Yes** to the question and close the Find Files window by clicking the **X** in the upper-right corner. Now somewhere on the Desktop, you should see a new AOL icon that is named Shortcut to AOL.EXE. Or, the icon will be named

Shortcut to <whatever the name of the .exe was> If you don't want that name, just follow the icon renaming instructions stated previously in this chapter.

Fig. 43 Right-click on the little icon that is found in the search and left click on Create Shortcut. Say Yes to the subsequent message and a shortcut will be created on the Desktop.

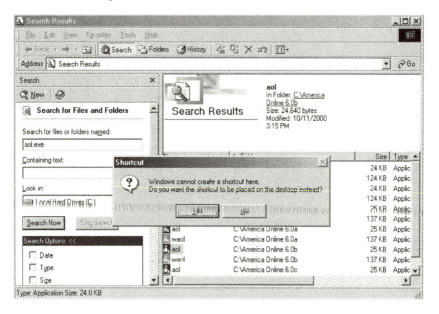

Now to break this up into digestible bits, I will continue right where we left off here in the next chapter. Also, if your brain is about to explode, call it a night or take a break and grab a cup of java or something. Then settle back for another cup of info.

Chapter #14

How to Move, Copy, Delete, and Rename files Part II

BRACE YOURSELF THE COMPUTER MAY CRASH

One thing you need to realize before juggling files around: If you move a file by dragging and dropping on the same drive, it will be moved. If you move a file by dragging and dropping from one drive to another, it will be copied. Your main drive is labeled drive C and your floppy drive is labeled drive A. Therefore, these are different drives. What we will be dealing with here is how to copy files from the hard drive, that is your main drive or C, to the floppy drive letter A. Why do I want to do this? you ask. Well, if for some reason your computer crashes and you need to reinstall Windows, you will lose all of the information that you have put into the computer thus far. In other words, it will revert back to the way it was when you first got the computer. So if you have been keeping your budget or your tax information on the computer, or you installed a game or two, or installed anything for that matter, those programs will be gone if you have to reinstall Windows. Now if you have any of these programs on a CD or floppy disks, you will not really lose the program itself, but you would have to reinstall them. However, those tax records would be lost forever!

If you used Turbo Tax, and you had it on CD, you could reinstall the program again. But what about your personal files that you created? Those didn't come on the CD, so they would be gone. Needless to say it's prudent to back up your files if it is going to be a catastrophe if they are lost. There are many ways to perform a backup these days, but the floppy disk is still prominent as a backup choice. The disadvantage of a floppy is that it just doesn't hold that much data; the capacity is a mere 1.44MB. We are going to start out small though, and floppy disks can be adequate to back up a lot of data in some cases. Let's say for example that you have 10 files in that tax program. As long as each of your files are smaller than 1.44 MB, you could put each file on a floppy. Even though this could take up to 10 separate disks, it would be feasible. And you could very well fit all 10 files on the same floppy. To put this in perspective, a rewritable CD-ROM will hold 675 MB. You can usually fit a lot of text files on 1 floppy disk. This entire chapter is just about 15 KB as a text file (.txt).

When I backed up this entire 2-volume book, it fit on 2 floppies. The Foreword through Chapter 18 fit on one floppy disk and chapters 19-25 fit on another, which didn't even take up the entire 2nd disk. I used a 3rd disk to back up everything else such as the appendices and the glossary.

There are 8 bits in 1 byte of computer data. Bytes are made up of 1s and 0s (ones and zeros). Every letter or numeral is made up of 1 byte. Therefore, each byte is made up of what is called a binary string of 1s and 0s. Every character that you can type is made up of a series of eight 1s and 0s, that are situated in a different order to represent each character. If you type a 6-letter word, you have used 6 bytes. There are 1000 bytes in 1 Kilobyte (KB). There are 1000 Kilobytes in 1 Megabyte (MB) and there are 1000 Megabytes in 1 Gigabyte (GB).

Compare ASCII and Binary files outlined **in Appendix E,** *Description of ASCII and Binary Files.* The binary strings of data are a little bit different between the 2 types of files.

I'm going to take you through creating a directory and then copying that directory on to a floppy disk. Right-click on the **Desktop.** Click on the Desktop wallpaper in an open area and not on any of the other icons. A right-click menu will ensue, and from that menu click on **New** and then

Folder. Hit the **Enter** key, and it will confirm your choice. A little review for you: Let's say that you want that folder to be named My Folder. Just rename it. Right-click it and left-click on **Rename**. Hit the **Delete** key on your keyboard and it will erase the name. Type in "My Folder" without quotes, and hit the **Enter** key to confirm your choice.

Fig. 44 Shows file was copied on floppy.
Notice that it remained on the
Desktop as well.

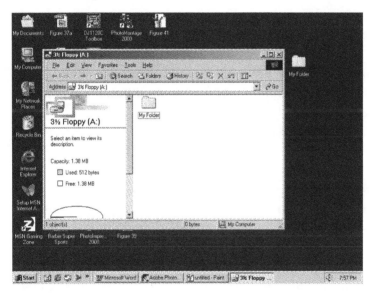

HOW TO COPY FILES FROM ONE DRIVE TO ANOTHER

Now we are ready to copy that file. Right-click on the folder that you just made called **My Folder** and then left-click on **Copy**. Now open up My Computer by double-clicking on it. In the upper-left corner, you should see an icon labeled 3 ½ floppy (A:). Insert a blank floppy disk into the floppy drive. Then, right-click on the 3 ½ floppy (A:) icon and this time left-click on **Paste**. The file will be copied, and you should hear the computer write to the floppy drive. Actually this file is so small, you probably won't be able to really tell if it was copied until you view the contents of the floppy drive. Double-click on the floppy (A:) icon, and a little window will open showing that your folder is there (see **fig. 44**). If you notice, it's still on the Desktop too which means that you copied it instead of moved it.

The rules I mentioned earlier about a file moving on the same drive and copying on a different drive don't apply if you use the right-click menu. That's the way to override those rules that only apply if you drag and drop a file. The point is that if you wanted to move the file to the floppy so that it did not remain on the Desktop, you do things the same way as before, but right-click and choose **Cut** instead of Copy. Of course you could always go back at the end and delete the file on the Desktop if you chose copy and didn't want the file to remain in it's original location.

The same principal can be applied to any file on the computer. You probably get the idea, but let's do one more. We will do a "real" file this time with some data on it so you can get the full effect of the copying process. When the file is sizable, you can hear the computer writing to the floppy disk, and you will see animated papers flying in the air symbolizing the moving or copying process. Let's open up the Windows Explorer and see what we can find.

CHECKING FILE PROPERTIES

Click **Start>Programs>Windows Explorer**. Look to your left and you will see all of the files on your hard drive (remember drive C). If you have America Online or CompuServe 2000, we will deal with one of those. If you don't have any of these, double-click on one of the directories on the left to bring up the contents of that directory on the right. Then just pick a file at random and copy it. One thing that we want to make sure of is that the file is smaller than 1.44 MB so that it will fit on a floppy. Here we come to yet another lesson within a lesson: How to check the properties of a file. The properties will tell you how large the file is. I will break this down into 2 sections to make it easier, and how to check the file properties will be explained. The first section will apply if you have AOL or CompuServe 2000. The second will apply if you have neither.

If you have America Online or CompuServe 2000:

Double-click on the directory to the left that is named America Online (it might say AOL something or America Online 5.0 or 6.0 or something similar). It will bring up the contents to the right. If you have CompuServe, double-click on the folder to the left that is labeled CompuServe 2000. Your personal files will be in a file called Organize. The Organize contains your address book, favorites, and anything saved in your personal filing cabinet. You won't be able to read any of this data except when you are in the AOL program, however. Check the properties of the Organize. Right-click on the file and left-click on properties at the bottom of the right-click menu. This page will show you the file size. If this is expressed in Kilobytes (KB), there will be plenty of room to put it on a floppy disk. If it is expressed in Megabytes (MB), just make sure it is not greater than 1.4 MB. If it is too large for a floppy, open up the Organize and you can copy your individual screen name. Don't forget to check the properties though, as this can be too large also to fit on a floppy if you have a large filing cabinet. You will see a file with yourscreen-name.arl, but just ignore that one. It just holds the history file and none of your information. This time we'll use the toolbar to copy the file. Last time we used the mouse commands. Click on your screen name file once to highlight or select it or click to highlight the entire Organize file if it's not too large. Click **Edit** on the menu bar and choose **Copy**. Open up My

Computer and click once on the 3 ½ floppy (A:) drive icon to highlight (select) it. Click **Edit** on the menu bar and click on **Paste**. whala! You should see files being thrown from one drive to another.

If you don't have any of these files I've talked about, just double-click on a directory on the left- hand side of Windows Explorer and start checking the properties on the right. The size 500 KB to 1.4 MB would be fine. A file size of at least 100 KB, and you will get the animated picture of the files being thrown from one drive to another as illustrated in **fig. 45**.

Fig. 45 Files thrown from one drive to another

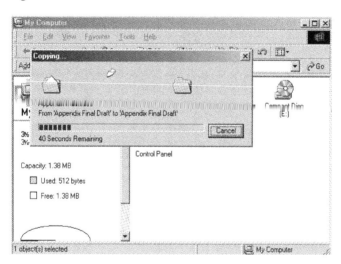

Chapter #15

How to Drag, Drop, Copy, and Move Files Using the Methods Discussed:

The premise of this chapter is a hard concept to grasp sometimes, but you can do it! The prerequisites in order to master this lesson are that you are good at single and double-clicking the mouse. You need to have mastered the right-click principle by this point as well. I think the biggest reason why people have trouble with these concepts is that most people simply don't realize that they can be done. For that matter the same holds true for many things on a computer.

TRANSLUCENT FOLDERS AND MOUSE POINTERS

Let's try something simple first: Create yourself a new folder on the Desktop, and we will drag and drop it to the recycle bin to get rid of it. First, right-click the Desktop in an open area (on the wallpaper and not on anything in particular) then left-click on **New** and choose **Folder**. You will have an icon that is named **New Folder**. Click on this with your left mouse button and keep the mouse button held down. Roll your mouse toward the recycle bin continuing to keep the button held down. You will see a translucent copy of this folder under your mouse pointer that will move with you. The original folder will still be on the Desktop as well—at least so far. Don't let the mouse button go until you are over the recycle bin icon and then release the left mouse button. A message will ask you if you want to move it to the recycle bin. Click on Yes, and your file will be deleted. You will no longer see the icon on the Desktop. See **fig. 46** for an illustration of a file being deleted in the recycle bin.

TIP Restore things from the Recycle Bin

You can retrieve things out of the recycle bin that you have deleted previously. Open up the bin and click on the item that you want to get back out. Click on File on the menu and click Restore.

The Recycle Bin lets you view items you've tossed in the same way as an ordinary Windows folder. If you're looking for something in the Recycle Bin, select Details from the View menu and click on the bar of your choice (Name, Original Location, Date Deleted, Type or Size) to sort by that category.

Fig. 46 File being deleted to the recycle bin.

MORE DRAG AND DROP

This procedure can be applied in virtually any area on the computer. That example is just about the most elementary drag and drop function that you can perform. Now let's copy a file from the hard drive to the floppy A drive by using drag and drop. Create a new folder on the Desktop again by using the procedure outlined before. Drag and drop the new folder in the lower-right corner of the Desktop by the system clock. Put it there so that when you open up My Computer, it won't cover the New Folder icon. Now Double-click on My Computer, and insert a blank floppy disk in the disk drive. Left-click on the New Folder icon that you moved in the lower-right corner of the Desktop. Hold your left button down and keep it down. Drag the file up toward the open My Computer window, and don't let it go until you are directly over the 3 ½ Floppy (A:) icon, and then let the mouse button go. It should promptly be copied to the 3 ½ Floppy (A:) drive. Check to make sure by double-clicking the floppy drive A. The folder that you dragged and dropped should be in the floppy drive contents window. See **fig.** 47 to see how it should appear.

Fig. 47   New Folder on floppy A drive.

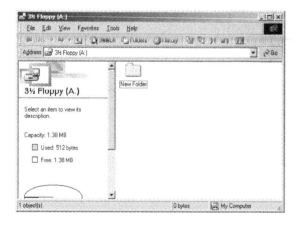

DRAG & DROP WITH THE RIGHT-CLICK MENU

Yes, indeed there are right-click drag & drop options on all Microsoft Windows versions after the Win 3.x series (Windows 3.1, 3.11—Windows for Workgroups, etc.). In other words, Windows 95, Windows 98, Windows Me, Windows 2000 and Windows NT 4.0 and above. A Microsoft mouse had a 2nd mouse button during the Windows 3.x era but there was no use for it. Well, actually that's not entirely true. There were right-click options in certain places, but only if the software was specifically designed with the functions for the right mouse button; they certainly weren't nearly as broad as they are in the later Windows versions.

Create a file on the Desktop by employing the same procedure as outlined at the beginning of this chapter. Drag your file from the Desktop to the floppy drive, but click and drag with your right mouse button this time. With this method, you can override the Windows defaults that copy a file from the C drive to the A drive. With the right mouse button, you will get the following choices on the menu. **Move here, Copy here, Create Shortcut here,** and **Cancel.**
These are fairly obvious, but I would like to elaborate on the Create Shortcut here. Try the following with a New Folder that you made on the Desktop or even any icon on the Desktop. You can experiment and then drag and drop the extra shortcut folders to the recycle bin afterwards. Right-click on the icon you choose and just drag it about an inch. Let go of the mouse button and choose Create Shortcut here. You will see an icon that is identical to the first one except it has a (2) after the name of the icon. If you create a shortcut to the 2nd shortcut, that icon will have a (3) next to the name and so on. This is shown in **fig. 48**. The shortcut is symbolized by the little curved arrow in the lower-left hand corner of the icon. Kinda cool isn't it?

TIP Get rid of the Recycle Bin's annoying questions:

Here's how to get rid of that annoying message that the Recycle Bin will ask every time you want to delete a file. Right-click on the Recycle Bin and left-click Properties. Uncheck the box that says "Display delete confirmation dialogue" and click Apply then OK at the bottom. From then on, you will not be prompted with the message: "Are you sure you want to remove the folder ... and remove all it's contents to the Recycle Bin?" every time that you delete a file. You can also uncheck the box that says "Do not remove files to the Recycle Bin. Remove files immediately when deleted." Be wary of this one—especially as a novice computer user. Once you delete a file, it is gone for good if you uncheck the do not remove files to the Recycle Bin checkbox.

TIP Get rid of the Recycle Bin's annoying faux pas:

Recycle Bin has an annoying habit of needlessly prompting users with "are you sure?" each time you attempt to deposit file refuse in it—even when you've unchecked the "Display delete confirmation dialog" on its properties screen. To workaround it, place a shortcut to the Recycle Bin in your \Windows\SendTo folder. To delete something straight away, just right-click it and choose Send To > Recycle Bin. You can also bypass Recycle Bin's protection entirely by dragging and dropping something to Recycle Bin, or by selecting the object for deletion and holding down the Shift key while you press the Delete button.

Fig. 48 A shortcut to a shortcut to a shortcut.

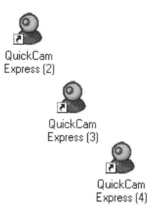

QuickCam
Express (2)

QuickCam
Express (3)

QuickCam
Express (4)

SHORTCUT TO MAKING SHORTCUTS

Remember in Chapter 13, *How to Move, Copy, Delete, and Rename Files,* we searched files and folders for aol.exe after foolishly deleting the Desktop icon? (Ok. here it is one more time ;-)
Click **Start>Find>Files or Folders** or **Start>Search>For Files or Folders** for Windows Me. Make sure the Look In box is set to the C drive. Type aol.exe on the Named line (Search for files or folders named line if you have Windows Me) or another executable file if you don't have AOL. Then right-click on the little icon on the left of the file that it finds when you do your search and click **Create shortcut here**. At that point you get a message that says "You cannot create a shortcut here, do you want to create a shortcut on the Desktop instead?" You say **Yes** and close the Find window. You will see your shortcut icon somewhere on the Desktop. If you don't see it—look again. If it really isn't there, try again because you did something wrong somewhere along the way.

The point I'm trying to make is that these are just shortcut's to the executable file within a program such as CompuServe, or Microsoft Publisher, or Quicken, or whatever. You can take the shortcut and drag and drop it across the Desktop and stop every inch or so and create many shortcut icons or more.

You can open up the Windows Explorer (**Start>Programs>Windows Explorer**) and open
up any directory on the left and drag and drop the executable to the Desktop (the executable is the file that ends in .exe or the one with the icon that symbolizes a certain program. For example, in AOL it is the AOL icon even though it may not show the file extension or .exe). You might want to shrink the Windows Explorer window so you can see the Desktop as illustrated in **fig. 49**. Dragging and dropping the executable to the Desktop will create a shortcut to the program.

Now you know just about all the ways to maneuver files around with the mouse button. One more thing to realize is if you right-click and drag the .exe file to the Desktop, you will get the usual right-click menu. If you left-click and drag an executable file, it will create a shortcut by default and you won't even have to click the menu selection that says **Create shortcut here.**

Fig. 49 Drag a file from Windows Explorer to the Desktop with Explorer shrunken to create a shortcut to an application.

COPYING FILES IN THE WINDOWS EXPLORER

In addition, there is something that you may have figured out already but that I failed to mention. In the Windows Explorer, in the far upper-left corner, it will list all of the drives that are in My Computer. They are just miniatures of the larger icons in the actual My Computer window that's accessible from the Desktop. You can drag and drop or use mouse click commands to move files from the C drive to the A drive, or the other way around, in the Windows Explorer.

Experiment with this if you like. You can drag files from the right-hand window across the vertical scrollbar that separates the 2 windows. Simply double-click on the C drive icon to bring up it's contents on the right-hand window. Double-click on a program like America Online, CompuServe, or anything else. Pick a file on the right-hand window side, and drag and drop it all the way back over to the left to the tiny 3 ½" floppy (A:). Experiment and have fun. Just remember that it would be a good idea to choose the **copy here** option if you are using the right mouse button, or copy the file instead of move it. That way if something goes wrong, you will have a backup of the file or it will not have moved from it's original location.

MAKE YOUR WINDOWS CLEAR

Furthermore, you can move the vertical scrollbar that separates the Windows in Windows Explorer. Just roll your mouse on the vertical bar until you see the mouse pointer turn into a double horizontal arrow. Left-click on it and drag it to the right or left and let go of the mouse button when it is in the location that you would like. You could partition the Explorer in half for instance by putting the bar right in the middle.

If you start copying a file to a floppy disk, and you don't check the properties first, it may end up being too large to fit. If the file turns out to be too large to fit on a floppy disk, it will still start to copy. However, it will tell you that there is insufficient disk space to continue when the disk fills up. When you click on **Ok**, none of that file will be copied.

If you copy a directory containing several or many smaller files that will fit on a floppy, it will copy files until the floppy fills up. Lets say you decide to copy the Program Files folder that may be 100MB or more to the little ole floppy disk. Obviously, it's not going to fit, but it could probably fit the first 6 or 8 files in the directory called Program Files onto the floppy disk. It will copy as many files as it can up until the point that the floppy disk is full and then you will see a message as shown in **fig. 50**. However, if it is just one file that is too large for a floppy disk, it will not copy any of it.

Fig. 50 A nice message will inform you to insert another disk if the first one fills up. Usually, if you have just 1 file that is too large for a disk, the message will come up right away informing you that there is insufficient space on the disk.

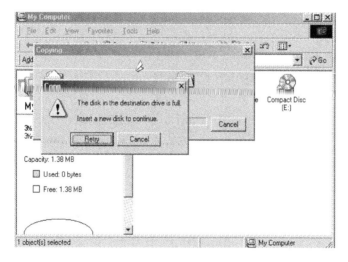

Moreover, you may run across a program that has a utility built into it that will copy the program from a CD-ROM to floppy disks. When the first floppy fills up, it will prompt you to insert another floppy disk; thus, the program can be continued from one floppy to the next. Ordinarily that cannot be done, but there are programs that will allow you to carry over a program on more than one floppy, and like I said, it is a feature you will see occasionally that is built into some applications. The main reason for this is either for backup purposes (in case you don't have a CD-Rewriteable), or you may have a 2nd computer without a CD-ROM drive at all. The option to copy to a floppy disk would allow you to install the same application on a computer with no CD-ROM drive.

Now we know how to Move, Copy, Cut, Paste, and create shortcuts. You are doing great! And by now you should be starting to get a feel for your computer and Windows. At least you shouldn't be so terrified of it. And with that said, Volume 2 of this book delves a little deeper into Windows and the Internet so if you want to learn more, be sure to read it. We go on to Chapter 16 *What's Up With All the Folders in the Windows Explorer?* The lesson is like I tried to make all of them: An independent chapter that can be informative by reading individually or in the numerical sequence in this book. But at the same time, I tried to put them in some sort of logical order; tried to not just mix them up in a hat and number them but make it so that if you read chapter #1, #2, #3, and so on without skipping any of them, it will maximize your memory retention by making the information a little bit easier to digest.

In some cases, one chapter directly elaborates on another one. Such as chapters 13 and 14. *How to Move, Copy, Delete,* and *Rename files* and *How to Move, Copy, Delete, and Rename files Part II*, respectively. Not entirely by coincidence, usually the further down you read into a chapter the more advanced it gets. You may be able to read just one paragraph and it is a lesson in itself. And every paragraph builds upon itself within each chapter. This is kind of like math. Do you remember in school how each lesson builds on the last one? Or, each lesson delves a little deeper, at least requiring what you learned in the last lesson to go on. The appendices go into greater detail about some of the information covered in this book. I tried to put an advanced or intermediate-advanced tip in some of them just in case you are reading this with some computer knowledge or you are just a quick learner or a curious person. With that out of the way, hopefully I will see you in *Compquest Volume 2.*

Epilogue

volume 1

By this point you should be a little more familiar with your computer. You may have learned all that you care to from volume 1, but if you want to delve a little deeper into the subject of computers and the Internet, you may want to check out *Compquest Volume 2*. In the next volume we take an in-depth look at the control panel, Windows Explorer, the Internet, e-mail, file attachments, computer hardware, and much more.

You can learn to use a computer if you try. The important thing is not to give up and not to be afraid of the machine. There's a lot of information about computers in case you didn't notice, but try not to let that over-whelm you. Just take it one thing at a time and one day at a time and absorb what you can. If you've digested at least most of the first volume—all 15 chapters—you have a good foundation to build on. I encourage you to pick up *Compquest Volume 2* because I truly believe that if you read both of them, you will be far ahead of the game. Furthermore, the 2nd volume will answer some questions that will undoubtedly arise in your mind after reading the 1st volume. Maybe I will see you in the next volume but whatever the case, thank you for taking the time to read this book. I sincerely hope that you learned a lot from it.

—Jay Lurie

About the Author

Jay is an English major from the University of North Florida and he now resides in the suburbia of Jacksonville, FL. After a stint in the Army and attending college, Jay was the Vice President of an interior design company. He left that position to pursue a career in the high-tech sector of business; he has been working for a large Internet provider for several years now and took up writing as a part time hobby.

Appendix Index *Volume 1*

A *What to do and What to Expect When Calling Tech Support* (Primer 2, Chapter 6)

B *Shortcut Keys for Windows* (Chapter 2, 11)

C *How to View Web Pages Offline* (Chapter 9)

D *Downloading Files From the Internet* (Primer 3)

E *Description of ASCII and Binary Files* (Chapter 14)

F *Our Take on All the Freebies* (Chapter 9)

G *Internet Explorer Keyboard Shortcuts* (Chapter 9)

H *Resources* (Chapter 5, 6, 8, 12)

I *Content Advisor* (Chapter 9)

J *File Extensions* (Chapter 7, Appendix G)

What to do and what to expect when calling tech support

Some of the following advice may seem rather abrasive, but it is simply some tips from my perspective as a technical support phone consultant. If you are offended by anything in this article, lighten up a bit and enjoy yourself a little more because you are much too uptight! I apologize in advance if you do find this piece offensive, but I am giving you the straight scoop from a tech support person's point of view, and I figure people will appreciate that. I provided over-the-phone tech support for a major ISP for several years, and I just want to inform people
who call tech support of what many phone representatives experience and what thoughts go through their mind on a daily basis. The following article outlines some things that you should know and realize before calling technical support.

Same thing different day

You can have the computer on and talk on the phone at the same time. As a matter of fact unless you have a very general question like "How much does your service cost?" it is a good idea to be in front of the computer with the computer on. I mean if you called your mechanic and you told him that you had a ticking sound under the hood, he would probably tell you to bring the car in the garage so he could take a look at it right? If you are talking to tech support via phone, you probably can't bring your computer into your tech support's "garage," so they rely on you to be their eyes and ears. Technicians are not psychics or else they would probably be taking phone calls on the psychic hotline. So just try to be in front of your computer when you call for tech support unless you are prepared to write down instructions or you want the technician to e-mail you instructions. Most tech support reps are busy and they have a lot of people waiting to talk to them; it is not fair to them or the other customers if they have to wait for you to boot your computer up when you could have had that done before you called. If you don't realize that you can have the computer on and talk on the phone at the same time, they probably aren't going to be able to give you instructions either. You probably won't be able to follow the instructions on your own in order to fix your computer. And with that said keep this in mind:

A modem is a device on your computer that dials out over a telephone line. There are a lot of new technologies on the horizon that may supersede the plain old analog modem, but right now the modem is still the primary means of hooking up to any ISP. Some high-speed connections are just not available in certain areas yet, or they are not affordable to the general population. A modem is pretty much just like a telephone except it's hard to think of it that way because it doesn't have a receiver. What the modem really does is it converts your computer's language into a format that can travel over the telephone wire, and your modem delivers information that it gets from the telephone line (information that comes from your ISP. i.e. what you see on your screen like Web pages.) and it converts it back to a language that your computer can understand. It modulates and demodulates information hence the name modem.

Unless you have an external modem, the only part of the modem that you can see is where the phone wire plugs into the back of your computer's tower so it's hard to think of it as a telephone but that's essentially what it is. Therefore, when you dial into your ISP, it is just like you dialed the same number on your telephone. If you dial a long-distance number to connect to your ISP guess what? It is going to appear on your phone bill just as if you had dialed it on your telephone. Furthermore, your ISP probably cannot tell you whether a certain number is going to be long-distance for you to dial or not. They do not have access to the same information as the telephone company, and they would need to be able to get into their database in order to tell you this. Your ISP is NOT responsible if you dial a long-distance number to connect to them. They are not the ones that can tell you if a number is going to be long-distance for you or not, and they will not be the ones to charge you if you do dial a long-distance number. So don't expect a credit from you ISP if the telephone company charged you for dialing a long-distance number. It is your responsibility to check with your local phone company and ask them if you dial such and such a number is it going to be long-distance in relation to you. All that your ISP will be able to do is to tell you what numbers they have available in your area to dial in with. To expect credit from your ISP because your phone company charged you is equivalent to calling your credit card company and demanding a credit because you accidentally clicked Yes on something that you shouldn't have on the Web and the company charged your credit card. It is just not going to work, and you probably won't get too far if you demand credit. Actually, you would have a better chance with the credit card company because they have certain guarantees that may entitle you to get your money back. Your ISP will not have these guarantees, and they will even have a disclaimer about the phone number issue in their registration agreement.

Along the same lines there are usually 2 places to plug a phone cord into the modem. If you have a laptop, there is usually only 1 place to plug a phone cord so it is hard to get confused there. Except there is something called an R-45 jack that you will see on a network card. This is where you would plug in Cat 3 or Cat 5 cable for networking, and the only reason I am mentioning this is because the R-45 jack looks like a standard R-11 phone jack, but it is slightly larger. Furthermore, some laptops (and even some Desktop computers) will come with a network card. There is only going to be one R-45 jack on the network card, and since there is only one R-11 jack on many laptop modems, this might create some confusion. For this article, I will assume that you have a Desktop computer with an internal modem with 2 places to plug a phone cord. There is a such thing as an external modem. Externals aren't in wide use anymore, however. Many laptops nowadays have an all-in-one modem and network card, so again that will cut out any possible confusion because you will only be able to plug the telephone wire into 1 place if you have one of these.

There will be 2 phone jacks in the back of the computer (on the modem). One is usually labeled Line and one is labeled Phone. To hook up to your ISP you need to plug one end of your phone line into the hole labeled Line. Sometimes it will be labeled Telco for telephone company. Whatever the case there is usually one hole labeled Phone and another one labeled something else. The telephone wire plugs into the hole NOT labeled Phone, and the other end of the cord goes into a working phone jack in the wall. The one labeled Phone may have a little inscription of a telephone on it, and the other one may have an inscription of what looks like the end of a telephone wire on it. Sometimes, the telephone wire inscription looks like a little battery. The hole labeled Phone is an optional convenience jack that gives you an extra place to plug in a phone. That way if the modem is taking up the only phone jack in the room, you can plug your phone into the phone jack on the computer so you can talk to tech support while the computer is on and you are in front of it. Get it?

Therefore, nothing has to go into the hole labeled Phone on the modem. It is just an option so you can plug in a telephone. The only thing that has to exist is one phone line that runs to the modem in the hole labeled Line or Telco or not labeled Phone, and the other end of the phone cord runs straight into the wall where you would ordinarily plug in a telephone. It is generally a good idea, if you are having connection problems, to run a direct line from the modem to the wall. If you route the wire through a fax machine, surge protector, caller ID box or anything else, it can cause significant line noise or interference and prevent your modem from dialing out. Also, you increase the complexity of the wiring when you start adding things and you have a greater chance of hooking it up incorrectly. If you can't connect to your ISP, try running a direct line from the computer to the wall and then you can start adding devices if you like. If it stops working when you route it through a surge protector, you either have the wires crossed or the surge protector isn't working properly. Or, the part of the surge protector where you plug a phone wire isn't working anyway. If you have a direct line and you get a "no dial tone" message, try plugging the phone cord into the other phone jack in the back of the computer before calling tech support. Sometimes the modem isn't labeled clearly or labeled at all or you may not be able to get in the back of your computer to tell the difference between the Line and the Phone ports.

Learn to walk before you can run

The next thing that you should do out of common decency before calling tech support is to go through some of the tutorials that are included with your computer. I mean I know that you are eager to get online and send and receive e-mail, and that may be the sole reason that you got a computer in the first place. But we have to walk before we can run right? Usually with Windows there is a tutorial that comes up right after you turn the computer on for the first time. Do yourself and your technician a favor: Take the 15 or 30 minutes and go through the tutorials. Or, at least skim the computer manual. This might even answer your question, but if not you will have a better understanding of this expensive machine that you just bought. People call tech support and they want to get online with their computer still in the box; that's kind of taking the cart before the horse don't you think?

Furthermore, if you have never touched a computer in your life, but you have a teenager in the house that could write programs for Microsoft, why not let them navigate the computer and you watch the 1st time that you call tech support? You'll come a long way in a short time if you watch someone that's good on a computer. If there is no one in your household that can call for support or you are the most knowledgeable, go ahead and call tech support. Technicians don't mind helping anyone that is really trying and receptive to instructions. But what really burns a lot of techs up (or out) is giving computer lessons.

TECH SUPPORT: Use it don't abuse it

Technicians are there to fix your computer and not to give you computer lessons. If your ISP offers free tech support, then the 20 bucks or so a month that you pay is for the service just like you might pay 80 bucks a month for your cable service. If your ISP tech support is free, use it as you need it and call as much as you like if you have a legitimate reason. Just don't take advantage of it and expect a tech to give you computer lessons. If you want lessons, pay someone to come to your house and give you lessons or get your teenage son or daughter to show you a thing or two. You see, the reality of the situation is that in most cases tech support people are under stringent time constraints. They have maybe 8 ½ minutes or so to solve your problem. If you have a legitimate problem and it takes an hour to solve, any decent tech will not leave you in the lurch. However, these people need to have an average talk-time of maybe 8-10 minutes. This is not their fault, but it is due to guidelines set down by the corporate office. At any rate, if you decide that you want
computer lessons and keep a tech on the phone for 30 minutes when it should have been an 8 minute call, it could cost that person his or her job regardless of how knowledgeable they are.

Take a chill pill

Try not to call tech support with an attitude. You catch more flies with honey than with vinegar. Most of the time calling with an attitude will get you no where except maybe a dial tone in your ear. Treat a tech with the same respect that you want and deserve, and you will get that respect back. The only reason that a tech may seem unfriendly or cut & dried is because probably he has talked to an irate person right before you or maybe several that day, and also he is under some pressure as far as the time that he can spend on the phone with any one call. I will tell you personally that I used to get calls all the time asking for general Windows help that had nothing at all to do with connecting to the ISP. I once had a guy call and he said "Look I know that this has nothing to do with you guys, but please help me I beg you!" "What's wrong?" I said. The customer said "I downloaded a nudie picture as my Desktop wallpaper, and I don't know how to get it off. My wife will be home any minute and I'm going to be in big trouble. Please help me!!" Guess what? I helped the poor guy get rid of his porno wallpaper. Another scenario could have gone like this: "Thank you for calling your ISP how can I help you?" "Yea I need to know how to get this nudie wallpaper off my screen." "Um sir I'm not going to be able to help you with that since it is unrelated to the service. You will need to call your computer manufacturer for that." "Bullshit! I pay you guys $20 a month for tech support. Now you're gonna help me!" "Unfortunately sir I can't since this is a Windows issue." "Let me speak to your supervisor then." Chances are the supervisor is going to say the same thing because they are going to go by the book. They are the ones that are supposed to uphold the tech support guidelines and remind the representatives of them if they start slipping and supporting things that don't relate to the service. I think I've made my point, and I'm not saying that anyone wants their ass kissed but just don't be a moron.

Remember that techs understand and empathize with your frustration. We have all been there many times. However, if a tech is worth his salt, he or she will do his very best to solve your problem. Believe me it's an ego buster not to fix someone's computer when that's what you do for a living. So when you've called tech support 10 times and you still have problems, it's not that everyone hasn't really tried to solve the problem. And if you think that you're frustrated, a tech listens to frustrated people for 8 hours a day and sometimes longer. You see with troubleshooting you have to try one or two things and see how that works before you go onto something else. Let's say that you can't get to the Internet. There could be 300 reasons why that isn't working. You call in and they make 3 or 4 adjustments and send you on your way to test it. It still doesn't work, so you call back and they try 3 or 4 more things and send you to test it again. If you have a really unique or difficult problem, you may have called in half a dozen times or more and you still aren't on the Internet. You finally call and demand a supervisor because you're really pissed off and with a reason to be. The other thing is, in most cases, a supervisor may not be particularly adept at fixing your problem. They are most likely there to keep track of the representatives and to run administrative interference between the tech and their own supervisor. The tech's supervisor may or may not know a lot about computers even, but they probably won't be more aware of the day-to-day problems that one may encounter than the tech himself that takes these calls day in and day out.

The trouble with troubleshooting

Troubleshooting involves doing the most likely thing that would fix a problem and then the 2nd most likely and so on. If all the conventional fixes have failed, you start trying things that probably wouldn't ordinarily fix the problem but that might fix it. And finally, if the problem still exists, you have to try things that you wouldn't do ordinarily, but since everything else failed you have to resort to unlikely fixes. It will seem to a tech support caller that everybody tells them to do something else. Well, because people have different personalities and different perspectives, the steps might be tried in a slightly different order, but they will generally be the same things tried in the overall scheme of things. In other words, one tech might think that the reason you can't get to the Web is because some adjustments need to be made in the Network Control panel, and another tech might check your RAM memory and hard drive space first. But both techs would probably have about the same general fixes in mind and do the same thing in the first 8 or 10 things that would be tried, but they just might be done in a different order.

In addition, they don't want to make 10 adjustments the 1st time because maybe all that needed to be done was fix #1 and #2. If that is the case, something that they did after that 2nd fix might actually break something else. Also, they would never know what fixed it if they did everything that could possibly be done for each problem right off the bat. Like I said though, very few if any techs will actually blow you off and not fix your problem on purpose. They also want to make customers happy, and they want to be able to fix all computer problems because they are after all—technicians.

Don't try to do your own thing. Remember that you are calling tech support for help, and you need to follow their directions if you expect to get your computer fixed. If they are trying to get you into the control panel and you end up on another screen, it is just going to make things more difficult for the tech and for you. If you want to do your own thing, try it before you call and when you get ready to submit to someone else's directions, then call the support line.

Honesty—not an autobiography please

Don't start off the call by telling your life's story. There are sometimes that a background is needed if you have an ongoing case that "nobody" can solve. However, most of the time the tech will have a database with at least enough information to get a gist of what your problem is and what has been tried. If they want any information they will ask you for it. When I took calls, most of the time, I really didn't care what happened prior to what the problem is. I want to know what happens right now when you try to connect or what the exact error message is that you are getting right now. On the other side of the coin, if you have made any changes to your computer, you should mention that to tech support. This doesn't warrant a 10-minute dissertation, but out of common decency you might mention that it worked until you moved the computer or you got a new hard drive or you downloaded a program or whatever. You cannot expect your problem to be solved if you are not honest with the technician.

An interesting phenomenon that I noticed was that most of the time people would tell me everything from the time they purchased the computer to the time they called me—and every painful detail in between. Most of the details were completely irrelevant, and if they had just spared the details and told me the error message or problem right from the start, I could have fixed it in like 5 minutes. On the other hand, people that should have mentioned more details usually didn't. I talked to a guy for 20 minutes before he casually mentioned that he had recently installed a new hard drive and made some other major hardware upgrades. He said, "I don't know if it makes any difference, but I just got a new hard drive." In these cases, I probably could have fixed the problem in half the time or less than it actually took, but it may have ended up being 20 or 30 minutes or more because they didn't mention a pertinent detail. When calling tech support, try and strike an accord between not enough information and too many details.

It's who you know if they tell you no

Don't gripe to the tech about the functionality of the program itself. Let's say you want to use a certain program in conjunction with your ISP and the tech tells you that it is not going to work. If you really are still in doubt, just call back and get a 2nd opinion. Maybe call a 3rd time if you are still skeptical, and if all 3 people tell you that it can't be done, you can rest assured that it is just not possible. There are so many different computers and programs out there these days that there is a good chance of incompatibilities between software and/or hardware. There are some things that just will not work even if it seems fairly simple to you. If a tech tells you that something is incompatible, deal with it. You can gripe all you want, but the tech is a virtual peon and can't just hit a switch and instantly make it work—believe me they would if they could. Don't waste your time or the technicians by barking up the wrong tree. If you are looking for a system-level change, ask how you can call or write the corporate office. This may still not effect a change or get whatever it is that you want done right away, but there is a lot better chance of getting something done by someone who makes the million dollar decisions than by an hourly employee. Remember too that your $20 a month doesn't even pay to have a programmer look at the programming code, so don't expect anyone to make a major change (recompile) to the actual software program. However, if enough people write the corporate office, you might just get what you asked for in the next version of the software.

In most technical support environments, the representative's supervisor doesn't even have the authority to make any major changes. For that matter the supervisor's supervisor doesn't have that kind of pull. Probably nobody in that call center can really get done what you want if it requires supporting something that they don't support. If your ISP is sizable, they probably have a call center (or several) and a headquarters. The corporate headquarters is where you will find the people that have the power to really make system-level changes. However, don't expect major changes to be done quickly. A change that you want done might require revamping the entire makeup of the ISP's software, and this may just not be possible—at least until the next version of the software comes out. Any large business these days cannot really please everyone. No matter what, if you have enough customers, you are going to displease somebody. What all major ISPs aim for (and I guess any large company for that matter) is to make as many people as happy as they can for as long as they can.

Maximize your minimum

If your computer doesn't meet the minimum system requirements to run certain software, don't complain to the technical support department about it. Get a new computer, upgrade your computer, or switch software or ISPs or do what you have to do, but you really don't have a legitimate beef with the tech support facility. They have minimum requirements for a reason, and most of the time they are much more liberal than they even should be. Minimum requirements set forth by Microsoft assumes that everything on a computer is in perfect working order and people run Scandisk and Defrag on a regular basis. That is often, or should I say usually, not the case. The requirements stated by Microsoft to run Windows is just the bare-bones minimum to scrape by. You may be able to run Windows under the generous conditions that Microsoft claims Windows will run under, but you probably won't be able to do anything else such as get to the Internet if you just meet the requirements. If you try and run any modern software with any system slower than a pentium processor and 16MB of RAM, it is like trying to pull a full semi tractor-trailer with a Volkswagen beetle—It's just not going to work.

When you assume…

Don't assume anything. If a tech asks you what screen you are on, don't read into it. He is asking you so that he knows where to go from there. Contrary to popular belief, they probably won't be able to see your computer screen. They may want the ISP software open or they may want you on the Window's Desktop. When they ask you what screen you are on just say "I'm on the Desktop" or "I have your software open" or "I'm on the screen with the Recycle Bin, My Computer and the Start button." This gives the tech a reference point to go from so he can say "OK, click on Start then Settings and choose Control panel." So if they ask where you are on the screen, don't say "Well, I can't have your software open because I only have one phone line." They didn't ask you that, they simply asked what screen is in front of you now.

Curiosity killed the cat

On the same token, don't be apprehensive about the whole thing. If you are a beginner, the tech is going to take you through some things that you no doubt never knew that you could do on a computer. Just sit back and follow instructions and let the tech do the work, and maybe by the end of the phone call you will have learned a thing or two. Don't question what he tells you to do simply because you think that it can't be done. Furthermore, do not question every little thing. You need to have trust in tech support. There was nothing more irritating to me then when someone said "Well now why are we doing this" or "Now what is this going to do." Well, it just might fix your computer is what it is going to do. If you know enough to fix it yourself, then do so and don't call tech support. If you need help, tech support is there to help you. I don't mind explaining if the person is honestly just curious about what steps we are taking to fix a certain problem. As a matter of fact, I made it a point to provide an explanation of what we where doing and why. But, there are some people that incredulously question every little move and that is very irritating.

What kind of a nerd forgets their password?

And one more thing. Don't be embarrassed when you forget your password. We've all done it and when you do tech support via phone you see all kinds of strange situations on a regular basis. It's no big deal. Don't be apprehensive when you are calling support. The reason that you are calling is because you don't know what you're doing or are stuck in a particular area. Chances are if you are reading this book, the tech on the other end may be a computer genius compared to you and he may be just a database jockey. But in any case, he or she is probably going to know more than you. Just let them do the work and act as their eyes, ears, and hands; just go with the flow and let them worry about the computer problem. Furthermore, the worst that can happen is that you have to reinstall Windows, which is really no big deal—even for you. No one can blow up your computer from a remote distance so really the worst anyone or yourself could do is damage Windows to the point where it needs to be restored. Perhaps the computer won't even boot anymore for instance. Don't be fearful. Techs are there to help and just make sure that you have any data backed up on the computer that you care about losing.

Shortcut keys for Windows

General Shortcuts

Operation	Key(s)
Bypass CD-ROM autoplay	Hold down Shift while inserting CD-ROM
Cancel dialog box	Esc
Cancel drag-and-drop	Esc
Capture screen to clipboard	Print Screen
Capture active window to Clipboard	Alt + Print Scrn
Choose command or option	Alt+*underlined letter*
Close program/window	Alt+F4
Command prompt bootup	Press F8 when Starting Windows 98 message appears
Copy	Ctrl+C
Cut	Ctrl+X
Delete	Delete or Del
Delete, no Recycle Bin	Shift+Del
Find files or folders	F3
Help	F1
Paste	Ctrl+V
Properties	Alt+Enter
Refresh	F5
Rename	F2
Shortcut menu	Shift+F10
Shut Down	Alt+F4 after all windows closed
Start menu	Ctrl+Esc or

	Windows key
Step-by-step startup Press	Shift+F8 at startup beep
Switch to another program	Alt+Tab
System menu	Alt+- (hyphen)
Undo	Ctrl+Z

Dialog Boxes

Operation	Key(s)
Cancel without saving	Esc
Checkbox on/off	Spacebar
Choose option	Alt+*underlined letter*
Click default (dark-rimmed) button	Enter
Click selected button	Spacebar
Cursor to end of line	End
Cursor to start of line	Home
Drop-down list (open)	Alt+down arrow
Next option	Tab
Parent folder (go to)	Backspace
Previous option	Shift+Tab
Scroll	up arrow, down arrow, Page Up, Page Down
Slider left/right	left arrow, right arrow
Spin box up/down	up arrow, down arrow
Tab (next)	Ctrl+Tab
Tab (previous)	Ctrl+Shift+Tab

My Computer

Operation	Key(s)
Back	Alt+left arrow

Close	Alt+F4
Close active and parent windows	Hold Shift while clicking
	Close (X) button
Copy selected item(s)	Ctrl+C
Cut selected item(s)	Ctrl+X
Delete, no Recycle Bin	Shift+ Delete
Find Files and Folders	F3
Forward	Alt+right arrow
Paste	Ctrl+V
Properties	Shift+Enter
Refresh	F5
Rename	F2
Select all	Ctrl+A
Up to parent folder	Backspace

Windows Explorer

Operation

Key(s)

Operation	Key(s)
Collapse expanded folder	left arrow
Parent folder	left arrow
Expand folder	right arrow
Collapse selected folder	Num Lock +—(minus sign)
Select first subfolder	right arrow
Expand all folder below current folder	Num Lock + *
Switch between left/right panes	F6

Program Shortcuts

Operation

Key(s)

Operation	Key(s)
Cancel	Esc
Close document	Ctrl+F4
Close program	Alt+F4
Copy	Ctrl+C
Cut	Ctrl+X
Delete	Delete or Del

End of document	Ctrl+End
End of line	End
Find	Ctrl+F
Help	F1
Menu	F10
New document	Ctrl+N
Open document	Ctrl+O
Paste	Ctrl+V
Print	Ctrl+P
Pull down menu	Alt + underlined letter
Replace	Ctrl+H
Save	Ctrl+S
Select All	Ctrl+A
Select item from open menu	*underlined letter*
Start of line	Home
Top of document	Ctrl+Home
Undo	Ctrl+Z
What's this?	Shift+F1

Drag-And-Drop

Operation	Key(s)
Cancel	Esc
Copy file(s) being dragged	Ctrl+drag
Create shortcut(s) to dragged item(s)	Ctrl+Shift+drag
Move file(s) being dragged	Alt+drag

Accessibility

Filterkeys on/off	Hold down right Shift key for 8 seconds
High Contrast on/off	Left Alt+Left Shift+Print Scrn
Mousekeys on/off	Left Alt+LeftShift +Num Lock

Stickykeys on/off   Press Shift 5 times
Togglekeys on/off   Hold down Num Lock
                                                     for 5 seconds

WinKey

Here's what you can use the Windows key for. It's key that's on newer
keyboards in between Ctrl and Alt

* WinKey + E = *Opens Windows Explorer*
* WinKey + F = *Opens Find*
* WinKey + R = *Opens Run*
* WinKey + Pause = *Opens System Properties*
* WinKey + D = *Maximize / Minimize all windows*
* WinKey + M = *Minimize all windows*
* WinKey + Shift + M = *Undo minimized windows*
* WinKey + Tab = *Flip between open apps in the taskbar*
*WinKey+F1=*Help*

Additional Keyboard & Shortcut Tips:

Utilize those numeric keys

You can use the number keys on the numeric keypad as single-click
keyboard shortcuts for launching your 10 favorite programs.

Start by pressing the Num Lock key if it isn't already on. Next, right-click on an existing program shortcut and choose Properties.

Open the Shortcut tab. Click once inside the Shortcut Key field, press the number key that you want to associate with the program, then click on OK. Repeat the steps for each application. For Internet Explorer, you'll have to make a shortcut to the Desktop icon first, then follow the same steps using the new shortcut. If your Num Lock key isn't turned on by default, check your system's BIOS setup for a Num Lock default setting.

Shortcuts at your fingertips

Your applications on the Start menu are just two clicks away.

Here's how to make them only one click away: Right-click on the Start button and select Open from the Context menu. Select all the shortcuts you want, and drag and drop all of them onto the Links toolbar.

Resize windows using the keyboard

You can move or resize open Windows applications by using only your keyboard. First, press Alt+Spacebar to bring up a menu. Press S, then use the arrow keys to resize the window. Press M and move the window using the arrow keys. Press Enter to keep the window change or Esc to return the window to its previous state.

View all drives at once

You can view the properties of a drive by right-clicking on the drive icon in My Computer and then left-clicking on Properties. This will tell you the free drive space for one thing. Here's a way to view the properties for multiple hard drives all at once. Open My Computer and select all your hard drives by holding down the Ctrl key and clicking on each drive. Next, right-click on any one of the drives and choose Properties from the drop-down menu that appears; Windows will create a single dialog with tabs for each drive. It also works for floppy, removable and mapped network drives.

Rapid Restart

Restarting Win9x is normally a four-step process (click on
the Start button, select Shut Down, click on the
"Restart the computer?" button and then click on OK). You can
make it a one-step process by creating an icon on your desktop
that restarts Win9x. Open Notepad and type @exit. Close the
document and give it a name with a .BAT extension. Now save
the file somewhere on your hard disk. Create a shortcut to the
file by using the right mouse button to drag it to the Desktop
and then selecting Create Shortcut(s) Here. Right-click on the
shortcut and select Properties. Click on the Program tab and
select the Close on Exit box. Now click on the Advanced button
and make sure "MS-DOS mode" is selected and "Warn before entering
MS-DOS mode" is not selected. Click on the OK button twice. Give
your new shortcut a unique icon and name. From now on, whenever
you double-click on the icon, Win9x will restart, no questions
asked.

Another restart

You can create a shortcut icon that will automatically
reboot Windows. In the Command line, or Target field, type:
C:\WINDOWS\RUNDLL.EXE user.exe,exitwindowsexec
Name the new shortcut Restart Windows.
Warning: This shortcut restarts your system without
confirmation, so only double-click on it when you're sure
that's what you want to do.

Eject a CD with your mouse

Right-click on the CD-ROM icon in My Computer and select
Eject from the Context menu to eject the CD from the drive.

Disable Auto Run on your CD-ROM drive

Hold down the shift key while inserting the CD-ROM
disk. Keep holding down the shift key for several
seconds. The CD disk will not play.

You can also disable the CD-ROM so when you place
a CD in the drive it won't automatically play.

Double-click on My Computer and then on Control Panel.
Open the System Icon, then click on the Device Manager
tab. Make sure there is a dot to the left of "view device by
type." Click on the plus sign next to the CD-ROM drive.
Right click on your CD-ROM drive and select properties.
Click on the settings tab and click on the check mark that
appears to the left of "Auto insert notification." This removes
that check mark. Click on OK and then again on OK. When
you restart the computer, it will no longer start any
CD-ROM disk you insert.

Assigning Shortcut Keys

You can assign a Shortcut Key Combination to any shortcut
icon, program, or file. The key combo will open your program
even if you can't see it, like from inside another program,
with a couple of keystrokes. Right click on any shortcut icon,
including the ones on the Start Menu, and choose Properties. Type
Ctrl+ (any letter) to assign the key combination. In Windows Me,
type a letter where it says Shortcut Key; it will automatically fill in
Ctrl+Alt+whatever letter you used. Then just click **Apply** then **Ok**
at the bottom. Don't make 2 shortcuts with the same key combination
and make sure the key combo is something you can remember.

How to view Web pages offline

When you make a Web page available offline, you can read its content when your computer is not connected to the Internet. The reason why this is advantageous is that you may want to read Web pages but do not want to tie up a phone line. You can specify how much content you want to be able to read offline. For example, you can download just a page or a page and all it's associated links; you can go however many layers deep that you want to. If you just want to view a Web page offline, and you don't need the very latest updates to its content, you can save the page on your computer. There are several ways you can save the Web page. You can save the text only or you can save all of the images and text needed to display the page as it appears on the Web.

To make the current Web page available offline

1. On the **Favorites** menu, click **Add to Favorites**.
2. Select the **Make available offline** check box.
3. To specify a schedule for updating that page, and how much content to download, click **Customize**.
4. Follow the instructions on your screen.

Note
- Before you go offline, make sure you have the latest version of your pages by clicking the **Tools** menu and then clicking **Synchronize**.

To make an existing favorite item available offline

1. On the **Favorites** menu, click **Organize Favorites**.
2. Click the page you want to make available offline.

3. Select the **Make available offline** check box.
4. To specify a schedule for updating that page, and how much content to download, click **Properties**.

Notes

- Before you go offline, make sure you have the latest version of your pages by clicking the **Tools** menu and then clicking **Synchronize**.
- You can also make Web pages available offline without adding them to your Favorites list, by saving the pages on your computer.

To save a Web page on your computer

1. On the **File** menu, click **Save As**.
2. Double-click the folder you want to save the page in.
3. In the **File name** box, type a name for the page.
4. In the **Save as type** box, select a file type.
5. Do one of the following:

   - To save all of the files needed to display this page, including graphics, frames, and style sheets, click **Web Page, complete**. This option saves each file in its original format.
   - To save all of the information needed to display this page in a single MIME-encoded file, click **Web Archive**. This option saves a snapshot of the current Web page. This option is available only if you have installed Outlook Express 5 or later.
   - To save just the current HTML page, click **Web Page, HTML only**. This option saves the information on the Web page, but it does not save the graphics, sounds, or other files.
   - To save just the text from the current Web page, click **Text Only**. This option saves the information on the Web page in straight text format.

Notes

- With **Web Page, complete** and **Web Archive**, you can view all of the Web page offline, without adding the page to your Favorites list and marking it for offline viewing.
- When you choose **Web Page, complete**, only the current page is saved. If you want to view Web pages and the pages they link to while offline, click **Related Topics** below.

Notes

- In previous versions of Internet Explorer, offline viewing was called "subscribing."
- If you used channels in a previous version of Internet Explorer, you can find them in the Channels folder in your Favorites list.

*Taken from Windows Me help files. Microsoft Corporation. Intro is changed, however.

Downloading files from the Internet

One thing that you need to realize is that downloading files from the Internet is different from downloading files from e-mail. The outcome is essentially the same: You transfer a file to your computer and execute it if it is an executable file (which we'll talk about more at the end of this article) or open it if your computer has a program installed on it that is capable of reading your file. However, you need to realize that downloading from e-mail and downloading from the Internet are really 2 different procedures.

With E-mail, you usually receive some sort of message, and the mail may or may not have a file attachment. Sometimes an e-mail may contain no other message but to tell you that a file is attached. To download the file you click the **Download** button or **Download Now** or whatever it is called in your e-mail program. It comes up with a dialogue box that asks you where you would like to download the file.

When you download from the Internet, you will normally get a message that asks if you want to *download the file to disk* or *open the file from it's current location*. If you download the file to disk, it is saved somewhere on your hard drive. You have to find it and click on it to start the installation or to open the file if it is not an executable program. If you opt to open the file from its current location, it will run automatically, and it saves you from having to find the file on your computer and execute it. If this makes no sense to you or you still don't have a full understanding of all of this, read on.

Perhaps you need a little background information to really grasp this concept. When you opt to download a file from either e-mail or the Internet, a dialogue box will pop up and you can choose where you want to download it to. When downloading from the Internet, you will only get that dialogue box when you choose the save to disk option. If you open the program from current location, it will open itself as I have mentioned and the file usually will automatically go into a folder on the C drive called My Download Files. The file will have a name on the line labeled File Name in the download dialogue box. You can erase this and name the file anything you want. Just type in there what you want to call it. At the top of this window there will be a drop-down list. This is where it says Save In: A drop-down list is where you can click the little down arrow looking symbol {▼} and it drops down several choices from which you can click on and select.

Whether you download from e-mail or the Internet, you will end up with the same window with the dropdown list—provided that you selected the save to disk option when downloading from the Internet. The dropdown list shows every drive on your computer, Desktop, and My Computer. The drives usually consist of 3 ½ floppy (A:), (C:) drive, and your CD-ROM drive that may be labeled D, G, M, Q or maybe even another letter. There will be any other drive that you may have on the computer, but these might be all of the choices except for Desktop and My Computer. Desktop will put the file on your main computer screen (The one that comes up when you first turn the computer on with all the icons, the START button, etc) and My Computer is just another way to access all of the drives on the computer, but you can't actually download anything directly to My Computer.

If you want to save your file to a 3 ½" floppy disk, put a blank floppy in the floppy drive. Choose 3 ½" inch floppy (A:) from the dropdown list in the download window. Type whatever you want to call the file where it says File Name (or leave it the way it is if the file name is acceptable to you) and then click the **Save** button, which will usually appear in the lower-right hand corner of the window. If you want to save the file to your main drive or C drive, choose (C:) from the dropdown list. This may be named something else like Harddrive (C:), HP Pavilion (C:), or 80917(C:), but the C will be in there somewhere.

The thing about the C drive is that it has a lot of subdirectories. You can drill down through these files and choose to save a file in one of the subdirectories on the C drive. You could even make a new directory just for this purpose. You can always save your downloaded files to this same directory so you always know where all of the files that you download are.

Instructions to make a directory:

Open up **My Computer** and double-click on the **C drive** or Hard Drive. Click **File** in the upper-left corner and choose **New>Folder**. This will produce a new folder named New Folder. It may be necessary to scroll down to the bottom of the entire window to see the one that says New Folder. You can promptly hit the **Delete** key to get rid of the name that Windows gave this folder and type in whatever you want to call it—maybe Downloads—then hit the **Enter** key to confirm your choice of names.

If you already hit the **Enter** key before renaming it and it won't let you back in where the name is, just rename the file yourself. Right-click on it and left-click on **Rename**. Hit the **Delete** key to get rid of the present name or just start typing and it will get rid of the name automatically. Type in what you want for a name and hit the **Enter** key to confirm.

You could choose **Desktop** from the download dropdown list. That way the file will download to the Desktop, which is your main computer screen. The Desktop is the screen that comes up when you first turn your computer on. You know, the one with all of the icons and the START button. Choosing Desktop makes it easy to locate your downloaded file because it will be right there where all of the other icons are. If you forget where you downloaded the file, you can choose the **Find Files** feature in Windows to find it. It is a good idea to make a note of the file name just in case you have to search for it using the Find Files feature.

Another way to make a directory is to right-click on the **Desktop** and left-click on **New>Folder.** The folder will have the name New Folder, but you can name this whatever you want. Right-click on the folder and choose **Rename.** Hit the **Delete** key on your keyboard to get rid of the name. Type in whatever you want to replace it with and hit the **Enter** key to confirm your choice.

How to use Find Files or Folders:

Click on **Start>Find>Files or Folders.** Where it says Named, type in whatever the name is of the file that you downloaded. This is why it is important to pay attention to the name of any file you download. You might even want to write this information down. Underneath the Named line, there will be a dropdown list labeled **Look In.** Select (C:) drive or My Computer if you can't find C drive or if you think that you might have possibly downloaded the file to another drive besides C. By choosing My Computer, you will tell it to look in ALL of the drives on the computer. Make sure the box is checked that says include subfolders. Now just click on **Find Now** on the right-hand side of this window, and a little magnifying glass will move around in a circle while it is looking. You may get a message right away that says, "There are no items to show in this view." As long as the magnifying glass is still moving around, just ignore this message. It should come up with your file at the bottom. After it is all said and done, if you get the message "There are no items to show in this view," the file does not exist on the computer if My Computer is selected where it says Look In. Or you misspelled the file name, or you downloaded the file to a floppy disk that is not in the floppy drive now. You might need to redownload the file and pay more attention to where it is downloaded. If your file is found, just click on the little icon to the left of the file name that will be located at the bottom portion of the window; the program should open or do whatever it is supposed to do. It will say something like 1 file found in the lower-left corner—of course provided that the computer only found 1 file on the whole system with the name that you specified.

How to search for files or folders with Win Me

If you have Windows Me, you need to click **Start>Search>For Files or Folders...** Type your search word where it says **Search for Files or Folders named**. All of the other principles, such as the Look In box are really the same as in olderversions of Windows. Just click on **Search Now** at the bottom when you areready to search for your file.

If you don't make a conscience effort to choose a download location, the file will download to a default location if you are downloading from e-mail. This will be wherever your mail program wants to put the file, which will usually be a designated download folder. Interestingly, if you choose "open the file from it's current location" when downloading from the Internet, by default it will download a copy of the file into the folder called My Download Files, located on the C drive. While it will start the installation automatically if you choose this option, it still
saves a copy so you don't have to redownload the file if you need to rein-stall the program.

What is an executable file?

An executable file is actually a self-contained program that has a specific purpose. It might be a game, a word-processor or office suite, a tax program, or a number of other things. There are many categories of programs these days. What I mean by self-contained is that it doesn't take another program to open these types of files. What defines an executable is that you can just double-click on the file or icon itself and the program will start running. Windows itself is the program that is actually needed to open an executable. Well, that's provided that the program is designed to run in a Windows environment, which most of them are these days.

Every file on a computer has a 3-letter extension. The extension on an executable is .exe. When you get a program on a CD, like say your ISPs program, it is an executable. That is why it installs if you double-click on the icon that represents the program; in most cases the CD-ROM drive is set up to auto run, so all you have to do is put the CD in and it will start automatically. Once that program is installed, you don't need the CD anymore (but you always want to keep it because you might need to reinstall your program some time in the future). The program is installed on your computers big drive (or C drive) at that point, so you don't have to put the CD in every time that you want to run that particular program.

If you download an executable file from the Internet, you just need to double-click on the program to kick it off, or if you choose "open from current location" it will start itself when the file is finished downloading. Open from current location would kind of be equivalent to putting a CD in the CD-ROM drive when auto run is enabled. In both cases, it will start to run the program automatically. So whether you install a program from a CD or download it from the Internet, you are just transferring an executable file to your hard drive. Once it is on your hard drive, it should not be necessary to redownload or reinstall the file unless the program becomes damaged or you reinstall Windows and lose all of your personal information on the computer. Furthermore, in most cases, you could copy the executable file from a CD to your hard disk. This is just a matter of copying a file from one disk to another. Your hard disk is kind of like several CDs stacked one on top of another. That way if your program became damaged, and you lost your CD, you would be able to reinstall without putting the CD in. Of course if you reinstalled Windows, it would erase the copy that you made of that file unless you copied it to a different drive other than C or you backed up your files.

There are many programs that offer you the option to do a partial installation. What this means is that it copies enough of a CD-ROM to your hard drive to run the program, but a lot of extra information is on the CD that is not copied to your hard drive. As you access that information, you will be prompted to insert the CD. Microsoft Publisher installed most of the program to my computer, but when I try to insert certain graphics, it prompts me to put the CD in so it can access that information. Programs such as Publisher would take up quite a chunk of hard drive space if you opted for the custom install and copied the entire thing to your hard drive.

If the file has another extension besides .exe, you will usually have to have a certain program that is capable of opening that particular type of file. Some programs you will probably have on your computer and some you won't. See Appendix J, *File Extensions* for a list of file extensions and what applications are needed to open them.

Description of ASCII and Binary Files

ASCII (TEXT)-stands for American Standard Code For Information Interchange. In simpler terms this is a computer standard for representing upper and lower-case Roman letters, as well as numbers and control characters on a US Standard 101/102 key keyboard.

ASCII files are commonly referred to as TEXT files or messages; they will appear in plain English such as the words you are currently reading. These types of messages do not require any special
type of program for reading, rather they can be viewed by a simple text editor.

BINARY- Binary files are basically defined as all non-ASCII files that consist of eight-bit strings of data (versus seven bit for ASCII). These types of files include programs, graphics, documents, spreadsheets, and all other such files that require a compatible type of program for viewing as the file was created with.

Our take on all the freebies

You want to know what I think of all the freebies? Well since you asked...

Quite honestly, I don't know what to think about all of these freebies abound on the Internet today. I mean this is rather unprecedented isn't it?

At what other point in history have so many things just been given away? In Medieval times, even before coinage, we paid for things with silver or gold or dealt with precious gems. Or, things were traded with goods or services.

The blacksmith might give the baker a set of horseshoes for some loaves of bread. Then there was the old West that worked in the same manner as in Medieval times except we had some sort of official currency. But were things just given away? I think not. That shot of bourbon at the local saloon cost a couple of bits. The tonic that the medicine man sold from his covered wagon cost money. Correct me if I'm wrong, but I don't think that those entrepreneurs gave their bottles of medicine away. Perhaps they did give small samples away just like some companies nowadays will mail out a small free sample. These types of freebies are different, however. When companies give away a small sample like that, they assume, based on a proven track record, that they will have some significant immediate (within a reasonable amount of time anyway) sales that come either directly or indirectly from the free samples. Back then money and riches had a different definition. Maybe your claim to fame would have been digging a gold nugget the size of a horse's head out of the side of a mountain instead of starting a dot com or throwing a good sum into Microsoft in the early 90s. But the principles remain

the same: There is no free lunch, a fair days work for a fair days pay, and a company has to turn a profit or it will go out of business.

At some point we went from the mom & pop stores to the dept. store model. Several people or more usually owned this new breed of retail entity. At what point in the timeline did this type of store start springing up?

Correct me if I'm wrong again, I'm no spring chicken but I'm a little bit young to remember when retail bricks & mortar stores pioneered, but these stores didn't have to give things away did they?

If they did have giveaways, it might be something like you get a free pumpkin for going to the store on Halloween. Or, maybe there were isolated giveaways or contests like we know today. A supermarket maybe would give away a turkey to the first 100 customers the day before Thanksgiving. But for a store to habitually give things away or have a long-standing free-for-all is an enigma.

Are they crazy?

I'll tell you that I never would have believed what is going on if I wasn't living in the midst of it right now. 10 years ago – 5 years ago – even a few years ago I would have thought you were clinically insane if you told me that
there would be legions of companies on the Internet that were giving things away for free!

I also have to be honest here. At first I couldn't grasp the whole concept of Internet freebies. I just couldn't conceive how in the world these companies could give things away. And we're not talking about 100 turkeys. With the traffic that's already on the Internet, most freebie sites have given away 1000s of whatever it is that they give away. Or, in the case of services, many of these sites have undoubtedly sunken hundreds of thousands of dollars into attracting mouse clicks. It wasn't too hard to figure out that advertising dollars were driving a lot of this generosity. There are many variations to this but basically company X pays company Y to put a link to them on their Web site. The more visitors company Y has, the more advertising bucks they can fetch from company X. So it makes sense to draw as many people to the site as possible, and what better way to do that then to offer something for free. But still all of these giveaways didn't make complete sense to me. This practice went against all business models that I've ever seen. I mean a business is in business to make a profit. This generally means selling products or services. Furthermore, fewer than 1 in 100 Internet banner ads are clicked through, and you know that a lot less than that are acted upon. These numbers of clicks that eventually lead to a sale will surely get less and less as the competition gets even fiercer.

Admittedly, I'm no mathematician, but something doesn't add up in this equation. These sites have to pay a staff plus ship the freebie in the case of a tangible product. Not to mention that there are some startup costs associated with getting a fully functional Web site up and running. Let's just assume that advertising bucks are covering the cost of the freebie giveaway. At that point they would break even, but you still have to cover everyone's salaries and the other operational costs of a Web site. How do they do it? The answer again is very simple: Venture Capital.

Hooray for the venture capital!

Venture Capitalists have put up millions and millions of dollars in a feeding frenzy on the Internet that has snowballed into epidemic proportions.

The problem is that even these large expense accounts will run out eventually if these fast startups don't figure out how to turn a profit. And what will the repercussions be if the Internet is taxed? I'll bet it will separate the men from the boys that's for sure. Will there be some sort of governmental regulatory commission for Web sites in the future? It's possible I think. At least there might be for sites that sell something. I think and hope that grandma and grandpa will always be able to post pictures of their grandchildren on the Web for free. But if we don't regulate the number of stores on the Web, eventually the competition could be overwhelming. Maybe it will cost a significant amount to start an online store, which would weed out some of the riff-raff. Maybe the industry itself and the economy will automate this for us. Ironically, it continues to get cheaper and cheaper to get a dot com to date.

We all learned in Economics class that competition in business is good. It is an advantage to the consumer and even the business for that matter. But what happens if there is too much competition? Would it spread things so thin that eventually it would force monopolies? Well we're getting ready to find out. Again, it is simple and intuitive to grasp that if you spend more money than you make, you will run out of money eventually. With that said, I think that eventually the party may be over. Or it may be he who laughs last laughs best. In other words, whoever is left standing after all the money runs out may be the winner by attrition. It's as hard to predict where all of this will end up as it is to predict what the stock market will do nowadays. I think that you'd better jump on the bandwagon while the iron is hot if you want to capitalize on all of the Web freebies though. After all, Venture Capitalists can only be so philanthropic. Most likely many of them will get sick of the red ink and cut their losses. I have been known to be wrong – once or twice a day – and hopefully I am wrong about this one. I hope that I have at least another good year to take advantage of all of these generous offers though I really do. I simply run out of time at the end of the day to visit freebie sites. As a matter of fact, I get so wrapped up with the day-to-day affairs that I rarely capitalize on any of the freebies that I have written about and listed myself. Of course, I do spend a good deal of time building Web pages and writing.

Web publishing is a hobby of mine, and it is something that I enjoy. I take pleasure informing the world about computers and freebies abound on the 'Net – just my little contribution to the world amidst all of these other freebies. An interesting point to ponder is that freebie sites keep a lot of the small timers, or people with no money, from setting up shop on the Web. How can someone compete in a category where there are freebies without having a lot of cash on hand? And if someone has that kind of money, might they just do something else with it like play the stock market? Someone would have to have a lot of nerve to try to sell mousepads when there is freemousepads.com, for example. Probably, it is just as well that all this mass funding has kept a lot of people from setting up an Internet company. There are far too many already if you ask me. What's funny is that you wouldn't know that a lot of people have probably been discouraged from starting a dot com because they don't have millions of dollars in Venture Capital. I mean there would be even more sites out there than there are already if everyone had their way. The scary part is that Web sites grow at an astronomical number of 1 every 5 seconds, and there is no end in sight. Everyone and their cousin has a site these days. Thank goodness they aren't all trying to sell us something!

On a different note

Allow me to seemingly step aside from the subject at hand for a moment. I think the stock market party may come to a close also. Somehow I feel that the market is associated with all of these freebies on the Web. They aren't directly related of course, but I feel that somehow the licentious run that some day traders have enjoyed will come to a close; the freebies brouhaha has the same feel to it as the bull market it would seem to me. The market may be up and freebies may be around for another year or two, but what goes up must come down is all I am saying. I'm not implying that the market will crash necessarily— although it's possible. I just think that the financial experts will find a way to circumvent e-trade and the like. They may recapture the market share, and take the big profitability out of the hands of the average citizen. And if they don't do it, the market itself might. There's one thing that we can be pretty sure of: There will never be a group of avant-garde financial analysts that run the whole stock market show like in the broker's heyday of the 80s as illustrated in such movies as American Psycho. However, a shift in the market could push a lot of people out of the game and maybe into bankruptcy; the winners will probably be decided by the timing and the avariciousness of the players. In other words, people that don't pull out in time, maybe due to greed, will lose big. There have been many people in recent times that have quit their day jobs in order to play the stock market. My father-in-law told me of some friends of his that were reluctant to spend $3500 on a software program that is supposed to pick the right stocks to invest in.

He said that they were very happy with their investment as they have been raking in $30,000 a month.

I don't know how many months in a row he was talking about. Also, I have a feeling that the people had some big bucks to put up front, but I didn't ask him all of the details. The bottom line is that I believe doom is eminent for many of these day-traders and a lot of the freebie sites; my mother always said, "Nothing very very good or very very bad lasts for a very very long time."

Internet Explorer keyboard shortcuts

You can use shortcut keys to view and explore Web pages, use the Address bar, work with favorites, and edit.

Viewing and exploring Web pages

Press this	To do this
F1	Display the Internet Explorer Help, or when in a dialog box, display context help on an item
F11	Toggle between Full Screen and regular view of the browser window
TAB	Move forward through the items on a Web page, the Address bar, and the Links Bar

SHIFT+TAB	Move back through the items on a Web page, the Address bar, and
	The Links bar
ALT+HOME	Go to your Home page
ALT+RIGHT ARROW	Go to the next page
ALT+LEFT ARROW	
or BACKSPACE	Go to the previous page
SHIFT+F10	Display a shortcut menu for a link
CTRL+TAB or F6	Move forward between frames
SHIFT+CTRL+TAB	Move back between frames
UP ARROW	Scroll toward the beginning of a document
DOWN ARROW	Scroll toward the end of a document
PAGE UP	Scroll toward the beginning of a document in larger increments

PAGE DOWN	Scroll toward the end of a document in larger increments
HOME	Move to the beginning of a document
END	Move to the end of a document
CTRL+F	Find on this page
F5 or **CTRL+R**	Refresh the current Web page only if the time stamp for the Web version and your locally stored version are different
CTRL+F5	Refresh the current Web page, even if the time stamp for the Web version and your locally stored version are the same
ESC	Stop downloading a page
CTRL+O or **CTRL+L**	Go to a new location
CTRL+N	Open a new window
CTRL+W	Close the current window

CTRL+S	Save the current page
CTRL+P	Print the current page or active frame
ENTER	Activate a selected link
CTRL+E	Open Search in Explorer bar
CTRL+I	Open Favorites in Explorer bar
CTRL+H	Open History in Explorer bar
CTRL+click In History or Favorites bars	Open multiple folders

Using the Address bar

Press this	**To do this**
ALT+D	Select the text in the Address bar
F4	Display the Address bar history

CTRL+LEFT ARROW	When in the Address bar, move the cursor left to the next logical break (. or /)
CTRL+RIGHT ARROW	When in the Address bar, move the cursor right to the next logical break (. or /)
CTRL+ENTER	Add "www." to the beginning and ".com" to the end of the text typed in the Address bar
UP ARROW	Move forward through the list of AutoComplete matches
DOWN ARROW	Move back through the list of AutoComplete matches

Working with favorites

Press this	To do this
CTRL+D	Add the current page to your favorites
CTRL+B	Open the Organize Favorites dialog box
ALT+UP ARROW	Move selected item up in the Favorites list in the Organize Favorites dialog box

ALT+DOWN ARROW	Move selected item down in the Favorites list in the Organize Favorites dialog box

Editing

Press this	**To do this**
CTRL+X	Remove the selected items and copy them to the Clipboard
CTRL+C	Copy the selected items to the Clipboard
CTRL+V	Insert the contents of the Clipboard at the selected location
CTRL+A	Select all items on the current Web page

Resources

1 Sweet, Lisa L. *Internet Computing Magazine* "Seeking Windows Compatibility," Volume 3 Issue 6. (chapter 5)

2 Spector, Lincoln *PC World* "Free Support Free-for-All" pgs. 139-146 *The best and the worst technical support study* p. 141 (chapter 6)

3 Scalet, Sarah D. *Pc Novice* GUIDE TO *Internet Basics* "**Your First Time Online—** What to Expect When You're On The 'Net," Volume 6 Issue 10 pgs 52-54. (chapter 8)

4 Carberry, Sonya *Smart Computing in plain English Windows Tips & Tricks Superguide* **"Windows File Systems—What You Need To Know About FAT16, FAT32 & NTFS,"** *Volume 6 Issue 6 pg. 62-64. (chapter 12)*

Content Advisor

The Content Advisor is a feature in the Microsoft Internet Explorer that enables you to require a password when accessing the Web to restrict access. Usually, this would be used as a parental control feature to restrict children's access to the Web. If you enable the Content Advisor, whatever you do, do not forget the password. Without the password, you will not be able to access the Web, and even deleting and reinstalling Internet Explorer will not resolve the problem. The reason why is that the Content Advisor writes the information to the Windows Registry, thus it needs to be removed from the Windows Registry in order to access the Web again if you forget the password. You will likely run into 2 errors concerning the Content Advisor that I have outlined below. I also included instructions to remove the damaged key from the Windows Registry if worse comes to worst. You need to be extremely careful whenever entering the Registry and I really wouldn't recommend it if you don't feel completely comfortable doing so. However, in a pinch you will save yourself $35 if you don't have to call Microsoft to resolve the problem.

—CONTENT ADVISOR CONFIGURATION INFORMATION IS MISSING OR DAMAGED

—CONTENT ADVISOR WILL NOT ALLOW YOU TO ACCESS THIS SITE

The reason why you may get either one of these errors is that the RATINGS.POL file or registry settings used by Internet Explorer are missing or damaged.

Check to see if the file is in the Windows\System directory

a. Click START on the START BAR.
b. Choose FIND.
c. Choose FILES OR FOLDERS.
d. Type RATINGS.POL in the NAMED: box. Verify that the LOOK IN box says (C:)
e. Click FIND NOW.

*If you have Windows Me, you need to click START>SEARCH>FOR FILES OR FOLDERS

*If the file is located in the Windows\System directory, it will need to be removed. Move it out of the directory and place it on the desktop for now or just click on it to highlight and hit the DELETE key on your keyboard to send it to the recycle bin if you have problems moving the file. If it is not in the directory continue to next step.

Recreate a new RATINGS.POL file

a. Click START on the START BAR.
b. Choose SETTINGS.
c. Choose CONTROL PANELS.
d. Double-click the INTERNET OPTIONS icon.
e. Click OK if the error message appears again.
f. Click the CONTENT tab.
g. Click the SETTINGS button.
h. If prompted for a password, type it in and hit OK.
i. Click the GENERAL TAB.
j. Click the option for USERS CAN SEE SITES WHICH HAVE NO RATING.
k. Click OK.

l. Click OK until Control Panels window is closed.
m. Verify that a new RATINGS.POL file is in the Windows\System directory using the FIND FILES option again.

*If the above fix does not fix the problem, you may need to contact Microsoft for directions on how to clear the damaged ratings key file from the Windows Registry.

Below are the instructions to remove the damaged key from your Windows registry. The registry controls the most rudimentary functions of your computer, and you absolutely do not want to make any changes in here except the ones specified below. If you are a computer novice, I really wouldn't recommend entering the registry. You may need to call Microsoft.

*Click **Start** on the Windows 95 Task Bar
*Choose **Run**
*In the Box type in **REGEDIT**
*Click **Run**
*Highlight **Hkey Local Machine**
*Click **Software**
*Click **Microsoft**
*Click **Windows**
*Click **Current Version**
*Choose **Policy**(it is possible that you will have to do this twice)
*Click **Ratings**
*Then Hit your **Delete Key** on your Keyboard.

This should take care of the Content Advisor Problem. If for some reason you are unable to follow these directions or any problems occur, contact Microsoft Technical Support.

MICROSOFT TECHNICAL SUPPORT NUMBERS

Standard Support Line
(425) 635-7000

Internet Explorer Support Version
(425) 635-7123

Free Support Line
(425) 635-7222 (**Mon-Fri 6 am—6 pm Pacific**)

File extensions

.$$$	temporary file
.@@@	Backup ID file
.000	Geoworks file
.2GR	286 Grabber Support File
.386	Intel 80386 processor specific file (Windows 3)
.3GR	386 Grabber Support File
.ABK	automatic backup file (CorelDRAW)
.AD	screen saver data (After Dark)
.ADF	Adapter Description File (IBM)
.ADN	Add-In Utility (Lotus 1-2-3)
.AFM	outline font description (Adobe Type 1 PostScript font)
.AI	Metafile (Adobe Illistrator)
.ALL	WordPerfect master printer file
.ANM	animation file (Deluxe Paint Animator)
.ANN	Help Annotations (MS Windows)
.APP	Application (R-Base)
.ARC	compressed file archive created by ARC (arc602.exe/pk361.exe)
.ARC	compressed file archive created by SQUASH (squash.arc)
.ARJ	compressed file archive created by ARJ (arj241.exe)
.ARS	Audio Resource File (WordPerfect)
.ASC	ASCII text file
.ASM	ASSEMBLY source code file
.ASP	Association of Shareware Professionals OMBUDSMN.ASP notice
.AVI	Audio Video Interleaved animation file (Video for Windows)
.AWK	AWK script/program
.BAK	backup file
.BAS	BASIC source code file
.BAT	batch file (DOS)
.BBS	Bulletin Board System announce or text info file
.BGI	Borland Graphic Interface
.BIB	Bibliography

.BIN	binary file
.BIO	OS2 BIOS
.BIT	bitmap X11
.BK!	document backup (WordPerfect for Win)
.BK1	timed backup file for document window 1 (WordPerfect for Win)
.BK9	timed backup file for document window 9 (WordPerfect for Win)
.BLD	BASIC Bload Graphics
.BKP	backup file (Write)
.BLK	temporary file (WordPerfect for Win)
.BMK	Help Bookmarks (MS Windows)
.BMP	BitMaP graphics file (Windows 3) (PC Paintbrush)
.BSC	Boyon Script (Boyon Communications)
.C	C language source code
.CAL	calendar file (MS Windows)
.CAT	Catalog
.CBL	COBOL Source Code
.CCH	chart (CorelChart)
.CDF	Comma Delimited File
.CDR	vector graphics file (CorelDRAW native format)
.CDX	Compact Index (Fox Pro)
.CEL	graphics file (Autodesk Animator)
.CFG	configuration file
.CGM	Computer Graphics Metafile vector graphics (A&L—HG...)
.CH	Header File (Clipper)
.CHK	recovered data file by CHKDSK (DOS)
.CLP	clipboard file (MS Windows)
.CMD	batch file (OS/2)
.CMF	Creative Music File sound file (Soundblaster command file)
.CNF	Configuration
.COB	COBOL language source code
.COD	Code List or Object List
.COM	command (memory image of executable program) (DOS)
.CPF	Fax (The Complete Fax)
.CPI	Code Page Information (MS-DOS)
.CPL	control panel file (MS Windows 3.1)
.CPS	backup of startup files by QEMM (?) autoexec.cps
.CPT	compressed Mac file archive created by COMPACT PRO (ext-pc.zip)
.CRD	cardfile (MS Windows)
.CRF	Cross-Reference File (MASM)
.CSV	Comma Seprated Value

.CUT	bitmap graphics file (Halo)
.DAT	data file in special format or ASCII
.DBD	Definition file (dBase)
.DBF	database file (dBASE III/IV—FoxPro— dBFast)
.DBG	Debug file
.DBK	database backup (dBASE IV)
.DBT	Datebase memo text (dBase)
.DBV	Datebase memo text (Clipper)
.DCT	Dictionary
.DEF	defaults—definitions
.DEM	demonstration
.DES	Description
.DHP	Dr. Halo Picture
.DIB	Device-Independent Bitmap graphics file (MS Windows)
.DIC	dictionary
.DIF	Data Interchange Format (databases)
.DIR	dialing directory file (Procomm Plus)
.DLL	Dynamic Link Library (Windows— OS/2)
.DOC	document text file
.DOS	text file containing DOS specific info
.DOT	Templet file (Word for Windows)
.DRS	Driver Resource file (WordPerfect)
.DRV	device driver eg. for printer
.DRW	Draw (Micrographics Designer)
.DTA	Data
.DV	Script (DESQview)
.DVR	Driver
.DXB	Drawing Interchage Binary (AutoCAD)
.DXF	Drawing Interchange Format (AutoCAD)
.EML	Electronic Mail
.ENC	encoded file—UUENCODEd file (Lotus 1-2-3— uuexe515.exe)
.EPS	Encapsulated PostScript vector graphics (Adobe Illustrator)
.ERR	Error file
.EXE	directly executable program (DOS)
.EXT	extension file (Norton Commander)
.FAQ	Frequently Asked Questions text file
.FAX	fax graphics image (WinFax Pro)
.FLC	animation file (Autodesk Animator)
.FLI	animation file (Autodesk Animator)
.FNT	Font file

.FON   font file (many—Windows3 font library)
.FON   log of all calls (Procomm Plus)
.FOR   FORTRAN language source code
.FOT   TrueType font file (MS Windows 3.1)
.FPT   Database memo text (Fox Pro)
.FRM   Report form file (x-Base)
.FRS   Font Resource file (WordPerfect)
.FXS   Winfax Transmit Format graphics file (WinFax)
.GBK   Back-up (Grammatik)
.GEM   Graphical Environment (Digital Resource)
.GEO   GEOS specific file (application) (GeoWorks)
.GIF   Graphics Interchange Format bitmap graphics file (CompuShow)
.GIM   Graphics link (Powerpoint)
.GIX   Graphics link (Powerpoint)
.GL   animation file (GRASP GRAphical System for Presentation)
.GLX   Glossary (MS-Word)
.GMF   Fax (GammaFax)
.GNA   Graphics link (Powerpoint)
.GNX   Graphics link (Powerpoint)
.GRB   MS-DOS Shell Monitor file (MS-DOS 5)
.GRF   Graph
.GRP   group file (MS Windows—Papyrus)
.H   Header: Include file (C)
.HDR   header for messages (mail) left by remote users (Procomm Plus)
.HEX   Intel Hexadecimal format file
.HLP   help information
.HPL   HP LaserJet
.HST   history file (Procomm Plus)
.HYP   Hyphenation
.ICO   icon (Windows3)
.ID   disk identification file
.IDX   index (many)
.IFF   Amiga Image File (Commadore)
.IFS   system file (OS/2) hpfs.ifs
.IMG   bitmap graphics file (Ventura Publisher—GEM Paint)
.INC   Include file
.INF   information text file (ASCII)
.INF   setup installation support file (MS Windows SDK)
.INI   initialization file
.INT   Object file

.JAS   graphics file
.JBD   datafile (SigmaScan)
.JPG   graphics file JPEG   Joint Photography Experts Group format
.JTF   Fax (JT Fax)
.LBM   bitmapped graphics file (Deluxe Paint/Amiga)
.LBR   Library
.LET   Letter
.LEX   Data files for spell checker (Word for Windows)
.LGO   startup logo code (MS Windows)
.LHA   compressed file archive created by ? (lha213.exe)
.LHW   compressed Amiga file archive created by   LHWARP
.LHZ   Compressed file (LHA)
.LIB   library file (several   programming languages)
.LOG   log file
.LRS   Language Resource file   (WordPerfect)
.LST   list file (archive index—compiler   listfile)
.MA   Program file (hDC Microapps)
.MAC   bitmap graphics   file (Macintosh MacPaint)
.MAP   Address map file
.MAX   Visioneer Paperport HP scanner file
.MCX   Fax   (Intel)
.MDX   Index file (dBase IV)
.ME   Opening Information (i.e.:   READ.ME)
.MEN   Menu
.MH   Fax (TeliFax)
.MID   MIDI file (MS   Windows)
.MKI   japanese graphics MAKIchan format (MagView 0.5)
.MNU   Menu
.MOD   Module file
.MOD   Sound file
.MPC   Microsoft   Project
.MPG   MPEG animation file
.MPP   Microsoft   Project
.MPV   Microsoft Project
.MPW   Microsoft Project
.MPX   Microsoft Project
.MRB   Multiple Resolution Bitmap graphics file (MS   C/C++)
.MSG   message text file (ASCII)
.MSP   bitmap graphics file   (MS Windows 2.x Paint)
.NDX   Index (dBase III+)

.NEW	new info
.OBJ	object (machine-language) code
.OLD	backup file
.OPT	Options
.ORI	Original
.OUT	Outlines
.OVL	overlay file (part of program to be loaded when needed)
.OVR	Compiler overlay
.PAK	compressed file archive created by PAK (pak251.exe)
.PAL	color palette file
.PAS	PASCAL source code file
.PC	text file containing IBM PC specific info
.PCC	cutout picture vector graphics (PC Paintbrush)
.PCD	Photo-CD Image graphics file (hpcdtoppm)
.PCL	HP Printer Control
.PCL	Freelance Graphics
.PCT	bitmap graphics file (Macintosh b&w PICT1—color PICT2)
.PCW	text file (PC Write)
.PCX	bitmapped graphics (PC Paintbrush)
.PDF	Printer description (Lotus, Borland)
.PDF	Adobe Acrobat file
.PFA	outline font description (Readable PostScript)
.PFB	outline font description (Adobe Type 1 PostScript font)
.PFC	text file (First Choice)
.PFM	Printer Font Metrics
.PGL	HP Plotter or Freelance Graphics
.PGM	PBM Portable Gray Map graphics file
.PGP	support file (Pretty Good Privacy RSA System)
.PGP	Program Parameter (AutoCAD)
.PHO	Phone list
.PIC	bitmap graphics file (Macintosh b&w PICT1—color PICT2)
.PIC	bitmap graphics file (many eg. Lotus 1-2-3—PC Paint)
.PIF	Program Information File (Windows 3)
.PIF	vector graphics GDF format file (IBM mainframe computers)
.PIT	compressed Mac file archive created by PACKIT (unpackit.zoo)
.PIX	Alias image file (SDSC Image Tool)
.PKA	compressed file archive created by PKARC
.PLL	Prelinked library (Clipper)
.PLN	spreadsheet (WordPerfect for Win)
.PLT	HPGL Plot File (Hewlett-Packard)

.PM	PM graphics file
.PNT	Macintosh painting
.PPT	Presentation table file (Powerpoint)
.PRD	Printer driver (MS-Word)
.PRF	Preferences (Grammatik)
.PRM	parameters (many)
.PRN	text file (Lotus 1-2-3— Symphony)
.PRO	Profile
.PRS	Printer resource file (WordPerfect)
.PS	PostScript file (text/graphics) (ASCII)
.PUB	public key ring file (Pretty Good Privacy RSA System)
.PUB	publication (Ventura Publisher)
.PUB	Microsoft Publisher file
.PW	text file (Professional Write)
.PX	Primary index (Paradox)
.QDI	Dictionary (Quicken)
.QDK	backup of startup files created by Optimize (QEMM)
.QDT	Data (Quicken)
.QIF	Quicken Interchange Format
.QLB	Library file (Microsoft Quick)
.QMT	Memorized list (Quicken)
.QNX	Index (Quicken)
.RAW	raw RGB 24-bit graphics file
.RC	Resource Script File
.REC	recorded macro file (MS Windows)
.REF	cross-reference
.REG	registration file (Corel programs)
.REM	remarks
.RES	Compiled Resource file
.RIC	Bitmap (Rhcoh)
.RLE	Utah Run Length Encoded rasterfile graphic file (SDSC Image Tool)
.ROL	Adlib Songfile
.RTF	Rich Text Format text file (Windows Word)
.RTF	Windows Help file script
.SAM	text file (Samna—Lotus Ami/Ami Pro)
.SAV	backup file
.SBB	Label definition file (Superbase)
.SBD	Definition file (Superbase)
.SBF	Data file (Superbase)
.SBK	Function key file (Superbase)

.SBM   Macro file (Superbase)
.SBP   Program file (Superbase)
.SBQ   Query file (Superbase)
.SBT   text editor file (Superbase)
.SBU   Update file (Superbase)
.SBV   Form file (Superbase)
.SCR   script (Kermit)
.SDF   Standard Data File
.SEA   Self-Extracting compressed Macintosh file Archive
.SET   Driver settings (Lotus) Image Settings (Paradox)
.SH   unix ASCII file archive created by SHAR (unshar.zip)
.SHK   compressed Apple II file archive created by SHRINKIT
.SHP   Bitmap (NewsMaster)
.SIT   compressed Macintosh archive created by STUFFIT (unsit30.zip)
.SLK   Symbolic Link format
.SMM   macro (Ami Pro)
.SND   digitized sound file (Macintosh/ATARI/PC)
.SNG   song (midi sound) file (Atari Cubase)
.SPL   print spooling file (MS Windows)
.SQ2   Compressed file
.STF   Structured File (Lotus Agenda)
.STY   Style
.SUM   Summary file (Grammatik)
.SUP   Supplemental Dictionary (WordPerfect)
.SWP   swap file (DOS)
.SYD   backup of startup files created by QEMM (?) autoexec.syd
.SYM   Synonym
.SYS   System file
.TBK   Toolbook
.TDF   Trace Definition File (OS/2)
.TFM   Tagged Font Metric
.TGA   Truevision Targa graphics file
.THD   Thread
.THS   Thesaurus
.TIF   Tagged Image File Format bitmap graphics (PageMaker—CorelDRAW)
.TLX   Telex
.TMP   Temporary file
.TRM   terminal settings (MS Windows)
.TST   Test
.TTF   TrueType Font file

.TUT   Tutorial
.TXT   text file
.UU   compressed ASCII file archive created by UUDE/ENCODE
.UUE   compressed   ASCII file archive created by UUENCODE (uuexe515.exe)
.VAL   Validity   Checks (Paradox)
.VBX   Visual Basic eXtension (Visual Basic)
.VGA   VGA display driver (many)
.VGA   VGA display font (many)
.VOC   audio   file (Soundblaster)
.VRS   Graphics driver (WordPerfect)
.VST   Truevision Vista graphics file
.WAV   Microsoft Waveform audio   file
.WDB   database (MS Works)
.WEM   Express Data File (hDC   Windows)
.WFM   graphics file (Corel Symbol & Typeface)
.WK1   Lotus worksheet R.2
.WK2   Lotus worksheet R.2x
.WK3   Lotus worksheet R.3
.WKB   document (WordPerfect for Win)
.WKE   Lotus worksheet R.1A   or MS-Works worksheet
.WKQ   spreadsheet (Quattro Pro)
.WKS   spreadsheet (Lotus 1-2-3 version 1A—Symphony 1.0—MS Works)
.WKZ   Compressed worksheet (Borland)
.WMF   Windows MetaFile vector graphics   (Windows 3)
.WPB   Button Bar (WordPerfect)
.WPD   Window Postscript   Description
.WPD   Document (WordPerfect versions 6 and up)
.WPG   WordPerfect Graphics Format bitmapped file (DrawPerfect)
.WPK   Keyboard   (WordPerfect)
.WPM   Macro (WordPerfect)
.WPP   Color Printing   Pallette (WordPerfect)
.WPS   text document (MS Works)
.WPX   Fax   (WorldPort, Fax Manager, JetFAX, OAZ Communications)
.WQ!   Compressed   Spreadsheet (Borland)
.WQ1   Spreadsheet (Borland)
.WQ2   Spreadsheet   (Quatro Pro 5)
.WR1   Symphony
.WRI   text file (Windows   Write)
.XLA   add-in macro sheet (MS Excel)
.XLC   chart (MX   Excel)

.XLM   macro (MS Excel)
.XLS   worksheet (MS Excel)
.XLT   template (MS Excel)
.XLW   workspace (MS Excel)
.ZLW   workbook (MS   Excel)
.ZIP   compressed file archive created by PKZIP or Winzip   (PKZ204G.EXE)
.ZOO   compressed file (Dhesi10/7/99 6:48 AM

*if your file isn't listed on this page, check out http://www0.delphi.com/navnet/faq/extguide.html or http://kresch.com/exts/ext.htm. Both are excellent references for file extensions, and the latter lets you search for the file extension.

Glossary

Accessibility Options—Applet in the control panel where you can make customizations to the keyboard, sound, display, and mouse to accommodate the hearing impaired and persons with other mobility and visual impairments.

Add New Hardware—**Applet in the control panel where you can install new hardware. You can let Windows search for the hardware or you can select the hardware driver from a list and configure it yourself.**

Add/Remove Programs—Applet in the control panel where you should go to safely uninstall programs. If you want to remove a program, it should be done through Add/Remove Programs if it is listed there. Add/Remove Programs also offers the option to make a boot disk by clicking on the Startup Disk tab; it can help you start your computer if it doesn't start normally. In Addition, the Windows Setup tab allows you to add components to Windows that weren't installed in the original installation such as Accessibility Options.

Adobe Acrobat—Application made by Adobe that is capable of reading PDF files. This program works cross-platform, on a Macintosh and an IBM compatible computer, and therefore, it is a widely used program. Another factor that adds to its popularity is because an Adobe file (PDF) will retain its formatting, look, and feel no matter what computer it is opened on as long as Adobe supports the operating system.

Active X—A program introduced by Microsoft that is used to instruct certain technologies how to involve COM (component object model) and OLE (object linking and embedding) functions. ActiveX can be incorporated within most programming languages. It lets Web site creators make interactive, multimedia Web pages and links to Microsoft Desktop products to the Web. For instance, through ActivcX controls, users could view Microsoft Word or Microsoft Excel documents through Microsoft Internet Explorer. Although the results of ActiveX controls may be similar to those of Java applets, Java is a programming language, while ActiveX is a set of controls written with Microsoft's Visual Basic.

ADSL—Asynchronous Digital Subscriber Line—High speed Internet connection that far exceeds the speed that an analogue connection can achieve. ADSL requires a special modem and a subscription from the telephone company. At the present time, ADSL is not supported in every calling area. Another advantage of ADSL is the ability to talk on the telephone and go online with only 1 phone line. **See DSL for another definition even though it is the same thing as ADSL.**

Advanced Technology Attachment Packet Interface (ATAPI)—An extension to the EIDE (Enhanced IDE) interface that supports CD-ROM and tape drives, which were left out of the original EIDE and IDE standards.

Advertising Banner—SEE BANNER

AOL—America Online—A popular online service that is known for its ease of use and convenience. AOL has a lot of proprietary online content that only AOL members can access. Because of the numbers of members that AOL has, they can often offer economic advantages on all types of goods and services.

Applet—A small application or utility, such as a mortgage calculator program, that performs only one task and is designed for use within larger programs. Because of their small size, many applets are available online as free software. They also may be easily incorporated into Web pages.

Application—A Program that can be installed on a computer to serve a certain function or functions. Most consumer software is applications that would include such things as games, word-processing programs, and spreadsheets.

Archie—Method of automatically gathering and indexing files on the Internet. This tool can sometimes be used to access FTP sites via Anonymous FTP (and download files) once it has zeroed in on the information that it searched for.

ARPANet—Advanced Research Projects Agency Network—A military project that started in the late 1960s that paved the way for the Internet as we know it today. ARPA consisted of many military computers networked together, and everything on the Internet was text-based at the time.

ASCII—American Standard Code for Information Interchange—The basic format that all text files are written in. It is a file comprised of 128 different code numbers that stand for the different characters in the alphabet. Any text file created with the DOS "edit" program is in ASCII format.

Asynchronous Digital Subscriber Line—See ADSL

ATAPI—See Advanced Technology Attachment Packet Interface

Attachments—Files that can be attached to e-mail and sent across the Internet. These files have a 3-letter extension that defines exactly what kind of file it is and what program is needed to interpret it.

Autoexec.bat—The abbreviated form of an automatically executed batch file. The Autoexec.bat file is a special batch file placed in the system's root directory that is automatically executed each time the computer boots.

Backbone—The main cable that has 11 interconnect points across the United States to which every network is connected to form the Internet.

Banner—Online advertising graphic. Usually located at the top of a Web page.

Basic Input Output System—(Pronounced bye-ose) See BIOS

Batch File—Text file that contains a list of instructions and is marked with the extension .BAT. When the file is run in DOS, each instruction is carried out in sequential order. A batch file can include any DOS command and can launch other programs.

Battery—A computer battery is round and it looks like a giant watch battery. It sits in a place on the motherboard and powers the system clock. It also maintains a steady trickle of energy that drives the system BIOS. On average, a computer battery will last 3-5 years and will need to be replaced.

Baud Rate—The rate at which your modem can send data. You will usually see this listed as BPS when you are buying a modem.

BBS—Bulletin Board System—A computer that allows you to call it and access a variety of functions. For example, many manufacturers have a BBS that contains recent software updates. If a customer needs them, they would call the BBS and download the files. The BBS is usually accessed via a Windows communications program called HyperTerminal. America Online has a BBS where you can download the latest version of their software; the number to call the AOL BBS is 1-800-827-5808.

Binary File—Any file that is not plain ASCII text. For example: executable files, graphic files and compressed (ZIP) files.

Binhex—Stands for BINary HEXadecimal, it is a method for converting non-text files (non-ASCII) into ASCII. This is needed because Internet e-mail can only handle ASCII.
See Also: **ASCII, MIME, and UUENCODE.**

BIOS—Basic Input Output System—Controls the input and output of the computer. Any information that is outputted from the computer or inputted to the computer is handled by this chip that is on the motherboard.

Bit—Single unit of information that has two values, 0 or 1 (contraction of binary digit).

Bitmap—Type of file format that is usually associated with the Paint program. A bitmap image is a rather detailed picture that normally has a large file size. Any bitmap can be used for an icon in Windows by simply renaming the bitmap with the icon extension (.ico).

Boolean—A standard system of logic that uses operators such as AND, OR, NOR, and NOT and is used to find information with search engines. To search for a document that includes the words "January" and "March," but not "February," the Boolean expression would be "January AND March NOT February."

Boot—The process of turning on the computer

BPS—**Bits Per Second**—Measurement of digital information transmission rates.

Browser—A software program that enables you to read Web pages; it is sometimes called a Web client.

Buffer—This is an area that is set up in memory to provide a faster way for the computer to process information; it holds recent changes to files and other information to be written later to the hard drive.

Bulletin Board System—See BBS

Bus—A physical pathway to connect internal peripherals such as video cards, modems and sound cards.

Byte—The primary unit of memory in a computer. A character is equal to one byte. In a byte there are 8 bits. Thus, each byte contains eight characters that are really different combinations of 1s and 0s.

Cable Modem—A device that uses a cable TV signal as a medium for connecting nodes on a wide-area-network. The main advantage of a cable modem is increased speed. Rates are a maximum of 56Mbps for data downloads, with a real-world rate of 3Mbps to 10Mbps. For uploads, the maximum is 10Mbps with a real-world speed of 200Kbps to 2Mbps.

Cache—(*Pronounced cash*) An area of memory that holds recently accessed information for faster retrieval the next time it is needed.

CD-ROM—A storage device that uses compact disks for read only storage. These devices use the same optical technology found in home stereo players.

Cell—The intersection of a row and a column in a spreadsheet, such as cell A1, the cell at the intersection of column A and row 1. Each cell is a box that can hold text, a numerical value, or a formula.

Central Processing Unit—See CPU

Channels—The path through which information flows from one device to another. This link can be either internal or external to the computer. Internally, a channel is more commonly called a bus. It is the physical link that facilitates the electronic transfer of digital information. A channel transfers information, for example, from the CPU to the keyboard. Externally, and typically in communications, it is a line or circuit that carries either analog or digital information, depending on the type of channel. Channel also can refer to an individual chat group using the Internet Relay Chat system.

Chassis—Part of the computer case. It is the backbone of the computer to which the motherboard, disk drives, and power supply are connected.

Client—Software that requests data from a server such as a newsreader, Web browser or FTP program.

Close Program Window—Accessed by pressing CTRL+ALT+DELETE on the keyboard. Close Program lists all of the programs currently running in the background and they can be closed one by one by clicking on a program listing to select it and click on End Task.

CMOS—Complimentary Metal Oxide Semiconductor—Storage area for your system BIOS. The BIOS writes the information that is entered into the CMOS setup in this special type of memory.

Cold Boot—The process of shutting the computer all the way down and turning it back on as opposed to a warm boot.

Complimentary Metal Oxide Semiconductor—See CMOS

Components—Components can be thought of as just a piece of a pie. When you say "a computer component," you are saying a piece of the computer that makes up the whole thing.

Config.sys—A text file that specifies the drivers and system parameters used in MS-DOS and OS/2. Config.sys controls some aspects of the operating system's behavior, and it contains commands about how to do things such as work with new hardware or adjust memory.

Conventional Memory—This is the first 640k of memory in your system (1024k=1MB). All programs must start in the first 640k of memory and then may use the rest of memory after starting.

Cookie—A method used by Web site operators to track visitors. Cookies are designed to recognize users' Ids or passwords when they revisit a Web site. After a particular Web server places the cookie on the computer user's hard drive, each subsequent request to the same server will contain that cookie.

Corrupt—To alter or partially erase information in memory or a file, rendering it unusable by the computer. Hardware or software failure can corrupt a file by rearranging the bits of data. Corrupted information is no longer readable.

CPU—Central Processing Unit—Also called the microprocessor. This chip acts as the "brains" of a computer. It controls the computer's actions and can find, decode, and carry out instructions plus assign tasks to other resources. Most IBM-compatible PCs use 386-, 486-, or Pentium class chips designed by Intel Corp.

Cursor—A visible indicator that tells you where you are positioned on the computer screen. The cursor is normally an arrow that moves around the screen as you move the mouse. You can have a custom cursor whereby you can make the symbol nearly anything that you want other than an arrow.

Daughter Card—A smaller card that plugs into a slot on the motherboard. Typically, a daughter card will serve as an expansion slot where other hardware cards can plug into. Some motherboards have what is called a riser card that is really the same as a daughter card; in either case, the card plugs into the motherboard so that it sits perpendicular to the motherboard. Other hardware, such as a sound card or ECP port may plug into the riser card.

DDE—See Dynamic Data Exchange

Dedicated Line—A communications line that is used solely for computer connections. A separate phone line that is used only so that your computer can connect to the Internet is a dedicated line. In other words, you may have 1 phone line that is used for normal phone calls and a 2nd phone line that is used for your computer.

Defragmenter—Disk Defragmenter is a Windows diagnostic program that should be run periodically; the more changes that you make to your file system (the more programs that you install and delete), the more often the defragmenter should be run. Disk Defragmenter closes the "holes" that are formed on the hard drive over time due to normal wear and tear. In addition, it rearranges the file structure and puts things into some semblance of order thereby allowing faster access to files by the hard drive.

Demodulate—The process whereby a modem translates an analog signal back into a digital signal that can be interpreted by a computer.

Desktop—The screen that comes up when a computer starts or is booted. The Desktop normally contains shortcut icons that point to the programs that are installed on the computer. Such things as the Start button, My Computer, and the Recycle Bin can usually be seen on the Desktop.

Device—Any component of your computer such as a printer, speaker, sound card, etc.

Device Driver—See Driver

Device Manager—Resides in the System applet of the control panel; it lists all of the hardware that is installed on your computer, and it allows for the manipulation and configuration of the hardware.

Dial-up Connection—The most popular way of accessing the Internet at present day. A dial-up uses an analog modem over POTS (plain old telephone lines) to connect to your ISP or the Internet.

Dial-up Networking—DUN—A built in feature of Windows that lets a computer connect to a network via a modem. It usually uses either the PPP (Point-to-Point Protocol) or SLP (Serial Line Internet protocol) to control the traffic between the computer and remote network. Windows 3.1 did not offer built-in DUN support. Instead, users had to obtain dial-up software such as Trumpet Winsock. Dial-up networking is almost exclusively used for connecting PCs to the Internet.

Digital Subscriber Line—Technology used to transmit digital data on regular copper phone lines. DSLs can be used to provide connections to the Internet or local-area networks (LANs) or for videoconferencing. The technology differs from Integrated Services Digital Network (ISDN) lines in that it can send analog and digital signals over the phone line. ISDN is digital only and has to convert analog voice phone calls to digital signals. With DSL, the analog voice phone calls and digital signals can coexist on the same wires. This works because analog signals require only a fraction of the capacity of the copper wires that make up a phone line. The limitation of the analog signal carried on those wires, not the wires, has kept phone lines from delivering greater data transfer speeds. Sending digital signals over copper wires breaks that barrier.

DIMM—See Dual In-Line Memory Module

Dip Switches—Tiny switches that allow for the adjustment of the IRQ and I/O port address of legacy equipment that are necessary for the manual configuration of hardware. Jumpers serve the same purpose; some hardware has jumpers and some may have dip switches. Generally, only very old hardware will have dip switches these days. You will still find jumpers on certain devices such as hard drives even in the plug & play environment.

Directory—A folder on a computer that can contain files. Microsoft dubbed a directory a folder to be less confusing to the consumer. Compare Root Directory definition.

Direct Memory Access—Addressing used by some hardware. Your system should have 6 available addresses 00 to 05. No two pieces of hardware can share a DMA channel. Most new hardware no longer uses a DMA.

Directory Path—SEE PATH

Disk Defragmenter—A diagnostic utility that is built into the Windows operating system. It rearranges files on the drive to put them in some semblance of order and to make them more quickly accessible to the CPU. Due to normal wear and tear, the hard drive can become fragmented over time. This means that files can be spread around the hard drive in pieces when they should be in one place. i.e. One program may be spread around the hard drive in several or more places. Disk Defragmenter puts all of the respective files that belong to each program back in one place, meaning that they can be accessed faster because the hard drive doesn't have to search around in many places to bring one file together.

Disk Drive—A device that accesses a disk for information.

Diskette—A magnetic object used to store files from a computer.

Disk Operating System—See DOS

DMA—See Direct Memory Access

DNS—Domain Name Servers—Computers that translate universal resource locators (URLs) to numeric IP addresses in order to facilitate Web browsing.

Domain Name—The unique name of a collection of computers connected to a network. On the Internet, domain names typically end with a suffix denoting the type or location of a site. For example, ".com" usually denotes a for-profit company; ".edu" an educational institution, ".gov" a government agency, and ".org" a not-for-profit organization. Country domains include ".jp" (Japan), ".cn" (China), and ".uk" (England).

Domain Name Servers—See DNS

DOS—Disk Operating System—Text only Operating System (OS) for a PC that requires DOS commands, or text-based commands, to operate the computer. DOS is the Operating System that preceded Windows. Windows greatest technological advancement over DOS is the GUI (Graphical User Interface).

DOS Prompt—This is a signal to the user that the operating system is ready to be given a command. You will see the DOS prompt as a letter followed by a colon, a backslash, and a greater than sign. (c:\>)

Download—To receive a file sent from another computer via modem.

Drive—A storage device that can be removable or fixed. A removable drive is something like a floppy or CD-ROM drive. A fixed disk is one that cannot be easily removed such as the C drive that holds all of the operating system files. Compare Hard Disk definition.

Driver—Also know as a device driver; it is a little program that allows for communication between the computer processor and a peripheral.

Drop-Down Menu—Menu on the computer where you select a choice instead of having to type something in. A drop-down can be characterized by a little down arrow (s) that you can click on to drop down several or more choices from which you can click on and select.

DSL—See Digital Subscriber Line

Dual In-Line Memory Module—A small circuit board containing memory chips. These boards are inserted into memory expansion slots to increase the amount of a computer's random-access memory (RAM). DIMMs differ from single in-line memory modules (SIMMs) in the width of memory bus supported.

DUN—See Dial-Up Networking

Dynamic Data Exchange—(DDE)—A two-way connection between multiple programs that let the programs actively exchange data while both programs are running. This exchange of data without user intervention is known as a conversation. Available with Windows and OS/2, this feature lets users use one program to manipulate data in another program. For example, if you use a communications program and a modem to connect to an information bulletin board, you can use a DDE to connect the incoming information to a word processing template for viewing. The incoming information may change, but the template will remain the same.

Dynamic-Link Library—An executable subroutine stored as a file separate from the programs that may use it. Dynamic-link libraries allow for the efficient use of memory because they are loaded into memory only when needed.

ECP Port—Extended Capabilities Port—Card that can be installed in a computer to expand its functionality. One example is a card that will add an extra parallel port to your computer. In that example, you could call the card a parallel port, but generally speaking, that card would be an ECP port also since it expands your computer by adding an extra parallel port.

EIDE—Enhanced Integrated Drive Electronics—Also known as Fast ATA (Fast AT Attachment), this is an updated version of the IDE (Integrated Drive Electronics) storage interface that works with hard drives and CD-ROM drives. It can shuttle data to and from the drive three to four times faster than the IDE standard (transferring data between 11MB and 16.6MB per second) and can support data storage devices that store up to 8GB more than IDE drives.

E-mail—Electronic Mail—Text messages sent through a network to a specified individual or group. Received messages are stashed in an inbox, and can be kept, deleted, replied to, or forwarded to another recipient, depending upon your E-mail program. Besides a message, E-mail can carry attached files so you can send word processing files or graphics.

E-mail address—Address used to send e-mail on the Internet. Normally, all e-mail addresses should be in lowercase with no spaces unless otherwise specified by the intended recipient. E-mail addresses are made up of essentially 3 parts: The first part is known as the username, screenname, or membername. After the name is an @ (pronounced at), and then the ending that is called the domain name. An example e-mail address is orion2400@aol.com. The domain name in that example is aol.com. Some large servers, such as those that may be found at universities or large corporations, contain another part after the domain name called a subdomain. An example e-mail address with a subdomain is metcalf@mit.edu.ras; ras is the subdomain in that example.

Embedded Graphics—Pictures that are inserted directly into programs such as an e-mail program. When a picture is embedded, it is opposed to a file attachment. Embedded graphics can be seen directly in a program such as e-mail; an attachment must be downloaded in order to view it.

Emoticons—Punctuation marks that are used in combination with one another to make symbolic representations of moods or thoughts. Usually an emoticon is some variation of a smiley, such as >:-(is an angry smiley; this is not necessarily true because punctuation marks can be used to create all sorts of imaginative designs. **Also see Smiley**

End User—You, the person that runs the computer.

Enhanced Integrated Drive Electronics—See EIDE

Expanded Memory—A type of memory that allows programs to use memory above one megabyte. This is for programs that are not capable of using extended memory by themselves.

Expansion Card—An expansion card is a device that is plugged into the motherboard to give the computer extra features. Examples of these are sound cards, modems, and video capture cards.

Expansion Slot—The connector that connects internal devices to the computer bus.

Explorer—This could be Windows Explorer or Microsoft Internet Explorer. The first one is a part of Windows that show you all of the files on the computer; it is accessed by clicking Start, Programs, and Windows Explorer. The latter is the Microsoft Internet Explorer Web browser.

Export/Import—A means of taking information out of the Registry and saving it as a text file in a format that can be put back in the Registry. Inputting this information is called Importing. This procedure is done by opening RegEdit clicking on the key you want to Export, then the clicking on *Registry* in the menu bar and then *Export*. It needs to be saved as a file without an extension. It should be saved within the Windows Directory so that you can Import it back if need be. To save the entire Registry, you click on *Computer* then *Export*. In general terms, Importing and Exporting can be done with many files among applications. For example, you may Import a picture into a graphics-editing program such as PaintShop Pro in order to manipulate the picture.

Extended Capabilities Port—SEE ECP PORT

Extended Memory—Additional memory above one megabyte.

External Modem—Unlike an internal modem, this is a self-contained device that sometimes resembles a cable box in looks and size. It performs the same function as an internal modem; because it is a separate unit from the computer itself, there is room for status lights that inform you of such things as whether the modem is transmitting data from the computer or receiving data from the telephone line.

Eudora—A popular e-mail program

FAQ—Frequently Asked Questions—Found on most Web pages, they are intended to answer the more obvious questions that may be asked about the content of a particular Web site. For example, if you go to www.winzip.com to download the WinZip program, you will find an extensive array of FAQs that will address all of the potential problems or concerns you may have about using WinZip except the most unusual circumstances.

FAT— See File Allocation Table

Fatal OE—Known as the Blue Screen of Death, it is when Windows becomes unstable and a blue screen appears on the monitor that tells you that a fatal error has occurred; it usually tells you to press a key to continue or in many cases you have to reset or shut down the system in order to clear the error.

FDISK—A Dos command and a utility in Windows that allows you to partition drives. Fdisk is cruder and a lot harder to use than commercial software that lets you do the same thing as fdisk but with a graphical interface. One such application is Partition Magic by PowerQuest that allows something as complex as partitioning drives to be a relatively easy task.

File—A collection of data that is stored as one unit.

File Allocation Table—Table information that is stored in the Data section of a bootable disk (floppy or hard). It normally consists of the first 63 sectors. Information about each file, size, location, and number of sectors used to store the file are kept there. If the table (Table 1) becomes corrupted, there is a backup table (Table 2). Windows uses Table 1 to read files, Scandisk for Windows can also read Table 2 if needed. Fdisk can read Table 2 also, if you use the MBR switch (fdisk/mbr) to repair the boot sector. If the Table becomes corrupted this is known as losing the FAT.

File Attachments—SEE ATTACHMENTS

File Format—All Windows files have a 3-letter extension that determines what format they are in. Some common file formats that are widely used across the Internet are GIF, JPG, and BMP. The format of a file determines what application is needed to open that file. Sometimes, it is necessary to have a particular program installed on your computer to read a proprietary file format or a file that is not widely accepted across the Internet.

File Transfer Protocol—FTP—A standardized, text-based method of transferring files over telephone lines from one computer to another. FTP often refers to a standard way of transferring many types of files over the Internet.

Firewall—A software and hardware implementation that protects an internal network from penetration and damage originating from an outside network. Also, a security model that allows a company to connect its internal network to the Internet—Allows for PUBLIC ("Sacrificial") and PRIVATE servers.

Fixed Disk—A disk such as a hard drive (C drive) that is permanent and cannot be easily removed. A fixed disk is in contrast to a removable disk. Compare fixed disk and removable storage media definitions.

Folder—A directory on a computer that can contain files. A folder will normally appear on a computer as a tiny folder icon that looks like a manila folder that you would use to store papers in a filing cabinet.

Font—The styles in which text appears. Some examples of fonts include, Times New Roman, Ariel, and Courier New.

Foreground Task—An operation or program that is being performed while another task is working in the background.

Formatting—This is the preparation of a diskette to be used for storage.

FTP—See File Transfer Protocol

Function Keys—The row of keys on top or on the side of the keyboard that are used for doing special tasks. (F1-F12)

General Protection Fault—When the operating system cannot process a command generated by a program it falters and cannot continue without dropping the command from memory. GPFs are displayed as an Illegal Operation something like Explorer caused an invalid page fault in module Kernel32.dll@01104:44455. This could be compared to a Fatal OE known as the Blue Screen of Death.

GIF—Graphics Interface Format—(Pronounced "jiff"). A method used to compress and transfer graphics images into digital information; it is commonly used to transfer graphics files on the Internet because of its excellent display of solid colors on all Web browsers.

Gigabyte—A unit of memory measurement that is equal to one billion bytes.

Gopher—Grouping of information servers throughout the Internet. Displays Internet documents and services as lists of menu options. If you select a menu choice, Gopher either displays a document (usually text only) or transfers you to a different Gopher system.

GPF—See General Protection Fault

Graphical User Interface—See GUI

Graphics Interface Format—See GIF

GUI—Graphical User Interface—The icons, graphics, toolbars and menu items that can be clicked on to perform functions on a computer. As far as an IBM-based machine, GUI first appeared in Windows 3.x; prior to that, computers were text-based. It was necessary to type cryptic-looking commands in DOS to operate an IBM machine before the graphical user interface.

Handshake—Noise that you will hear if your modem speaker is not turned off that represents the modem negotiation with a remote computer. A handshake sounds like a screeching noise that comes from data bits being shoved through the copper telephone wire as well as modulation and demodulation.

Hard Disk—A "hard" platter that stores mass amounts of information for extended periods of time.

Hardmodem—Modem that does not require software to be running all of the time in the background to function. They usually have their own processor or power and are not dependent on the power of the computer's Central Processing Unit (CPU). Compare a softmodem.

Hardware—Any peripheral of the computer that are tangible. Examples of hardware include the keyboard, modem, sound card, video card, mouse, and hard drive.

Hashed Password—A password encrypted with a very simple cipher that is easily broken if the password is picked up in transmission.

Helper Applications—Essentially browser plug-ins. Plug-ins were called helper applications in older versions of Web browsers.

History—A folder in the Windows directory that contains a trail of where you have been on the Web. Hence, you will usually find that there is a list of WWW addresses in the History folder.

Home Page—Document intended to serve as an initial point of entry to a web of related documents. It is also called a Welcome page. Contains general introductory information, as well as hyperlinks to related resources. A well-designed home page contains internal navigation buttons, which help users find their way among the various documents that the home page makes available.

HTML—Hypertext Markup Language—A language used to create electronic documents, especially pages on the World Wide Web, that contain connections called hyperlinks. Hyperlinks allow users to jump from one document to a related document by clicking an icon or a hypertext phrase. For instance, you might jump from a company logo or name on a Web page to the company's home page on the Internet.

HTTP—Hypertext Transfer Protocol—The set of standards that lets users of the World Wide Web exchange information found in Web pages. Web browser software is used to read documents formatted and delivered according to HTTP. The beginning of every Web address, "http://", tells the browser that the address' document is HTTP-compatible.

Hyperlink—An icon, graphic, or word in a file that, when clicked with the mouse, automatically opens another file for viewing. World Wide Web pages often include hyperlinks that display other Web pages when selected. Usually these hyperlinked pages are related in some way to the first page. Hyperlinks include the address or names of the files to which they point, but typically this code is hidden from the user.

Hypermedia—Combination of hypertext and multimedia on a Web page.

Hypertext—Also know as HTML, it is a type of text that allows embedded links to other documents. Clicking on or selecting a hypertext link (hyperlink) summons another document or section of a document to appear.

Hypertext Markup Language—See HTML

Hypertext Transfer Protocol—See HTTP

IDE—Integrated Drive Electronics—A standard in computer engineering that has since turned into Enhanced IDE. IDE has one channel on which 2 drives can be installed. EIDE added another channel so that a total of 4 drives could be installed on a computer. IDE can't move data as fast as its enhanced counterpart and it can't support as large of drives either.

I/O Port—An address given to a computer component. This address is specific to only that one component and no other. It is kind of like a street address. Your neighbor and you do not have the same address just as computer components don't have the same I/O port.

Illegal Operation—Error message that may be seen on a Windows-based computer. It does not mean that you have done anything wrong, but it is the way that Microsoft worded the message in the programming code that makes it sound somewhat intimidating.

IMAP—Interactive Mail Access Protocol—A standard Internet e-mail protocol that has superceded POP protocols. The POP (Post Office Protocol) is still widely used, although a lot of newer mail clients support IMAP as well.

Integrated Drive Electronics—SEE IDE

Interrupt Request Line—(or IRQ or Interrupt)—An interrupt is an address given to computer components like an I/O address. Unlike the I/O port, not every computer component has an interrupt.

Internet—The global Transmission Control Protocol/Internet Protocol (TCP/IP) network linking millions of computers for communications purposes. The Internet originally was developed in 1969 for the U.S. military and gradually grew to include educational and research institutions. Today, commercial industries, corporations, and home users all communicate over the Internet, sharing software, messages, and information. The most famous aspect of the Internet is the World Wide Web, a system of files saved in Hypertext Markup Language (HTML) format.

Internet Backbone—Communications networks that tie together the various infrastructural components that make the Internet work. These high-speed data lines are the fastest and most direct routes for Internet data to travel, and they carry the most Internet traffic.

Internet Options—Applet in the control panel where you can adjust all of the possible settings for the Microsoft Internet Explorer Web browser.

Internet Connection Wizard—A component of Internet Explorer that walks you through setting up your Internet connection.

Internet Protocol—See IP

Internet Relay Chat—See IRC

Internet Service Provider—See ISP

Integrated Services Digital Network—See ISDN

InterNIC—Internet Network Information Center—A private agency responsible for registering World Wide Web site domain names.

Interrupt Request Lines—Hardware lines over which devices can send signals to get the attention of the processor when the device is ready to accept or send information. Typically, each device connected to the computer uses a separate IRQ. There are 15 IRQs available. No two pieces of hardware can share the same IRQ, with the exception of your IDE controllers. These are usually 14 and 15. A special card can be installed in your machine to make more IRQs available.

IP—Internet Protocol—The address of a computer on a Transmission Control Protocol/Internet Protocol (TCP/IP) network. IP addresses are written as four groups of numbers (each group may consist of as many as three numbers) separated by periods. An example of an IP address is 118.173.113.13.

IRC—Internet Relay Chat—A type of interactive communication on the Internet in which computer users engage in real-time communication.

IRQ—See Interrupt Request Lines

ISDN—Integrated Services Digital Network—A telecommunications network that allows digital voice, video and data transmissions. ISDN replaces the slow and inefficient analog telephone system with a fast digital network. ISDN lines can transmit data at 128Kbps. Special equipment is required to connect to ISDN lines, which may soon become as affordable as other communications services.

ISP—Internet Service Provider—An organization that lets users dial into it's computers to connect to its Internet link for a fee. ISPs generally provide only an Internet connection, an e-mail address, and maybe World Wide Web browsing software. You can use an ISP based in your town that offers an access number in your local calling area or a national ISP that provides local-access numbers across the country. You also can connect to the Internet through a commercial online service, such as America Online or CompuServe. With this kind of connection, you get Internet access and the proprietary features offered by the online service, such as chat rooms and searchable databases.

Jazz Drive—A removable storage device medium that has a high-storage capacity. Disks available for a Jazz drive hold either 1GB or 2GB, respectively. It is not industry standard, meaning that a Jazz drive must be installed on a particular system to be able to
read the removable disks.

Joint Photographic Experts Group—See JPEG

JPEG—Joint Photographic Experts Group—(Pronounced "jay-peg") A color image graphics compression format in which a lossy compression method is used and some data is sacrificed to achieve greater compression.

Jumpers—Little electrical prongs that allow for manual configuration of a legacy device. Little plastic caps can be positioned over metal prongs in various combinations that determine the interrupt request and the I/O address of a device. These were mainly in use before plug & play prior to Windows 95. They are still on some hardware such as hard disks where you position the jumpers one way to make the drive a primary and another way to make it a slave drive.

Juno—A fully-featured Internet Service Provider. They once had a free e-mail program that is still in use today. The free e-mail service is somewhat antiquated compared to today's standards, however; it offers nothing but e-mail at a 9600 baud connection.

Keyboard—The typewriter-like input device that is used with a computer. A standard keyboard has 101 keys, and there is a number pad on the far right-hand side that resembles a calculator.

Keyboard Commands—A series of either 2 or 3 keys that can be pressed simultaneously on the keyboard to invoke a particular function. For example, the CTRL+ESC keys pressed simultaneously will bring up the Start menu, and pressing the CTRL+ALT+DEL keys twice in rapid succession will warm boot the computer.

Kilobyte—1024 bytes of data

LAN—Local Area Network—A group of computers that are joined in some way, usually by a physical cable, in order to share resources such as printers, scanners, and files.

Laptop—A portable computer that can either be plugged into an electrical source or it can run off of a battery for a limited amount of time before the battery needs to be recharged.

Legacy—The way that hardware was classified before plug and play. Legacy devices needed to be manually configured by adjusting jumpers or dip switches in contrast to plug and play whereby the computer generally detects the device itself and an installation wizard walks you through the process of setting up the hardware.

Local Area Network—See LAN

Lynx—A Web browser like Microsoft Internet Explorer or Netscape, but Lynx is not that widely used. Like the Opera browser, it tends to have a niche group of users.

Macintosh—Type of computer and operating system that rivals Microsoft Windows. It is not nearly as widely used as Windows, but it has grown in popularity to the point where it has a major foot hold in the computer industry. The Mac OS is more widely used in end user environments than any other operating system save Microsoft Windows.

Macros—A series of keyboard and mouse actions recorded to a single key, symbol, or name. Macros are helpful when you perform a task often.

Mailer Daemon—An automated response that is sent out via e-mail from a mail server; it does not come from a human being, but it is a computer-generated response that you will usually receive if your e-mail was undeliverable.

Mail Header—In e-mail, a header lists what mail server or servers the mail has passed through from point A to point B. In other words, it tells you where the e-mail originated from and where it was sent to and everywhere in between.

Mainboard—SEE MOTHERBOARD

Manufacturer—Companies that actually make computers. Some examples of large well-known manufacturers include Hewlett Packard, Gateway, Compaq, and Dell.

Math Co-Processor—A chip that is used to increase the speed of math functions. It is designed to handle the majority of math computations so the CPU can handle all the rest of the processing.

Megabyte (MB)—A measure of information totaling one million bytes (technically 1,048,576 bytes). This is commonly used to show size of hard disks, amount of memory, and the size of files.

Memory Address—A space that is allocated to processes on your computer. Each process is allocated its own address; when you get a message that a program has performed an Illegal Operation, two processes tried to occupy the same space at the same time and thus bumped heads. An analogy to memory addressing would be a parking lot. Each car has its own space where it can park; when two cars try to pull into the same space at the same time, it would be equivalent to a GPF (Illegal Operation) on a computer.

Memory Allocation—*Windows uses the random access memory (RAM) and a virtual memory address (Swap File). Windows places information into RAM and then moves it to the Swap File when it needs to make more room in RAM; it moves the information into the Swap File that is not needed immediately.*

Memory Manager—A program that tries to maximize the utilization of memory by the computer.

Memory Resident—A program that is loaded but not currently functioning. You can usually access this program by pressing a combination of keys like ALT-TAB.

Menu Bar Item—The words that are printed across the top of a window above the Toolbar. These usually include at least File Edit View and Help.

Metacrawler—Popular search engine that is technically a multi-search engine meaning that it has the ability to search many search engines at once.

Microprocessor—Also called the CPU or Central Processing Unit; it is essentially the brain of the computer that controls all of the hardware, and how fast the computer can perform operations depends on the speed of the Microprocessor. The speed is expressed in Megahertz (Mz) such as 800Mz.

Microsoft Internet Explorer—Microsoft's popular Web browser that is integrated into Windows 98. Windows 95 could function without Internet Explorer, but for all practical purposes Explorer has to be included in Windows 98 in order for Windows to work properly. Therefore, it can't be easily removed from Windows 98 like it could with

Windows 95. The only other browser that comes close to Explorer's popularity is the Netscape browser, running a distance second to Explorer.

Microsoft Network—See MSN

Microsoft Outlook—Popular e-mail program; a condensed version, called Outlook Express, comes integrated with the Microsoft Internet Explorer Web browser.

MIDI—Musical Instrument Digital Interface—Device that bridges the gap between a musical instrument and a computer. With a MIDI and the right software, you can perform such tasks as automatically making sheet music that reflects the notes that you play on an instrument.

Mime—Multi-Part Internet Mail Extensions—Because there is no Internet standard for e-mail yet, sometimes when you attach several files at one time to e-mail, the Internet e-mail system may encode the file attachment in MIME format to facilitate its transfer across the Internet. Essentially, the Internet may compress all of the files into one MIME file (.mim extension), and it is necessary to have an application that is capable of decoding or decompressing the file in order to be able to view it.

Minimize—You can minimize any Windows on a Windows operating system by clicking the – sign in the upper-right hand corner of a window. This shrinks it down to the Taskbar, usually located at the bottom of the screen, and you can maximize the window again simply by clicking on its icon on the Taskbar.

Modem—Acronym for *mo*dulator/*de*modulator. The device that lets a computer transmit and receive information over the telephone lines by converting digital data from computers into analog data that can be transmitted over phone lines. The opposite process takes place on the receiving end. Modems are the primary way computer users connect to outside networks, such as the Internet.

Modulate—A modem modulates information so that it can be sent over a standard telephone line. In other words, a modem converts digital data to an analog signal so that the data can be transferred via a phone line.

Monitor—Also called the screen or CRT, this is the output device that allows you to view what your computer is doing. (Hint: It looks like a TV)

Motherboard—This is the foundation of your computer. Everything in the computer is attached in some way to the motherboard by a cable or connector. The motherboard also houses the CPU and memory.

Mouse—A device that can be rolled across a flat surface to position the cursor on the computer screen. A mouse normally has 2 buttons—the left one controls all of the elementary functions that can be performed by either a single-click or a double-click. The right mouse button will produce a drop-down list where some specialized functions can be performed. A mouse may have 3 buttons; the 3rd button can perform even more specialized functions. There are other special features that you can find on some mice such as a wheel on the top that can be used to scroll documents or a track ball, a ball that you roll on top of the mouse to position the cursor instead of pushing the mouse around on a flat surface.

Mouse Pad—A place mat that you roll a mouse on to improve the traction of the ball on the bottom of a mouse that controls the cursor movement. A mouse pad generally has a rubber-like surface to maximize the traction.

MSN—Microsoft Network—An Internet Service Provider that is owned and operated by the Microsoft Corporation.

Multimedia—Multimedia is a description of anything that uses more than one media to achieve a desired effect. In the real word, an example of multimedia is a movie theater that uses picture and sound to achieve its desired affect. In the world of computers, multimedia would be the use of sound, pictures, video, and voice to achieve a desired affect of entertainment or education.

Multitasking—Running two or more programs at the same time.

Musical Instrument Digital Interface—SEE MIDI

National Science Foundation Network—See NSFNet

Netiquette—Slang for the unwritten rules of Internet courtesy.

Netscape Navigator—Popular Web browser that is still a distance second to Microsoft Internet Explorer, however many people use both Netscape and Explorer.

Network—A set of conjoined computers that can share storage devices, peripherals, and applications. Networks may be connected directly by cable connection or indirectly by telephone lines or satellites and can be part of a small-office system or a global web of numerous other networks.

Network News Transfer Protocol—See NNTP

Newsgroup—A group of messages about a single topic. On the Internet, newsgroups bring together people around the world for discussion of shared interests.

Notepad—A simple word processor and text editor that is included with the Windows program. It is very rudimentary, but it is effective to do simple tasks, like type a letter, when you don't need to do a lot of fancy text formatting.

NNTP—Network News Transfer Protocol—Industry standard protocol for the distribution, inquiry, retrieval, and posting of news articles to newsgroups on the Internet.

NSFNet—National Science Foundation Network—A network that was originated circa 1980 that consisted of mainly academics and scientists. This network joined with ARPANet, beginning the Internet as we know it today.

OCR—See Optical Character Recognition

Online Services—Any number of electronic forums that can be accessed via a modem. Examples of these are Prodigy, America Online, and CompuServe. On them you can receive a variety of information and can chat with people all over the world.

Opera—A Web browser that sort of has a niche user group.

Operating System—A complex set of instructions that tell a computer and its hardware how to function. Operating systems include Windows, MAC OS, Linux, Unix, and OS/2 as well as many others.

Optical Character Recognition—The process in which the images of letters, entered into a computer with a scanner, are translated into characters that are worked with in the computer as text, not as an image. OCR is far from perfect, but it is a fast method for digitizing typed pages of text. Some computer fax applications also use OCR to transform incoming faxes from graphics files to word processing documents.

Outlook—Popular e-mail program made by Microsoft.

Parallel—Type of port to which most printers and some external components are connected. Parallel ports transmit data 8 bits at a time.

Parallel Port—A card that fits into a slot on the motherboard that houses a parallel cable that might come from a printer or scanner. In other words, where the other end of your cable from a printer plugs into is going to be the parallel port.

Partition—A portion of the hard drive that is formatted to hold data. A hard drive may just have one partition or more; partitions can be formatted using several different drive structures such as FAT, FAT32, or NTFS.

Patch—A piece of code inserted into software to temporarily fix a defect. While most users do not consider a patch as a shortcut or a shabby way to fix a problem, adding too many can make a program difficult to maintain. Programmers often create patches to fix problems and add features to a program during the timeframe when users are awaiting the release of a new version of the program that already includes the "patched" corrections and new features.

Path—This defines exactly where a file, folder, or directory is located on a drive of the computer. For example, if there were a text document called letter.txt on the hard drive in a folder called Mytextfiles, the path to the text file would be C:\Mytextfiles\letter.txt.

Pegasus—An e-mail program, like Outlook, but it is not that widely used.

Peripheral—Any physical device connected to the computer.

Physical Memory—This is the Random Access Memory (RAM) on a computer. You can view the physical memory by clicking on Help then About Windows in the My Computer window.

PIM—Personal Information Manager—Program that helps users get more organized. PIMs often include calendars, telephone lists, and programmable reminders that are easy to use. Some PIMs included in operating systems or office suites also can be purchased separately. Some of the best-known PIMs include Microsoft Schedule+ and Starfish Software's Sidekick.

Ping—DOS command that will tell you how long it takes for a signal to pass from point A to point B on the Internet.

Pitch—Number of dots per inch used as a measure of typed characters.

Pixel—The smallest part of an image that a computer printer or display can control. An image on a computer monitor consists of hundreds of thousands of pixels, arranged in such a manner that they appear to each be connected. Each pixel on a color monitor comprises three colored (blue, red, and green) dots. The term comes from the words picture element and also is abbreviated PEL (Pronounced *pell*).

Plain-Vanilla ISP—An ISP that offers a connection to the Internet and that's it. A no frills ISP that may include an e-mail account and but no more. These are generally harder to use than an online service because they don't offer the handholding that a lot of the online services have.

Plug & Play—The user-friendly hardware installation that came about with Windows 95. Prior to that time, hardware was known as legacy; it was necessary to manually configure legacy hardware with jumpers or dip switches to make them work on a system. Plug & play means that you can usually just plug hardware in, boot the computer, and the installation is automated by the operating system.

Plug-Ins—Software that expands the features of main programs and adds multimedia capabilities to Web browsers. A plug-in is a small program that "plugs into" a large application and runs as a part of that application.

Point-To-Point Protocol—See PPP

POP—Post Office Protocol—A protocol that manages your Internet mail until you pick it up from your ISP.

POTS—Plain Old Telephone Service—Acronym that defines an analog connection as opposed to a high-speed connection such as a cable modem.

PPP—Point-To-Point Protocol—A communications language that lets users connect their PCs directly to the Internet through their telephone lines. Considered more advanced than the Serial Line Internet Protocol (SLIP) connection it is quickly replacing, PPP offers more error-checking capabilities as well as several forms of password protection.

Port—A connector that allows peripherals to be connected to the computer.

Portal—A site on the Web that offers a wide variety of resources, such as new articles, and services, such as e-mail, Web site hosting, and online shopping. Online services such as America Online were the first portals. Traditional search engines and computer giants such as Netscape and Microsoft are currently positioning themselves to take advantage of the interest in portals.

Postmaster—In the Internet world, the person that is responsible for handing the flow of mail for a domain. A Postmaster is an actual human being whereas Mailer Daemon is a computer-generated response from a mail server that is generated when e-mail is undeliverable.

Private Key—The secret half of a two-part public key encryption system. The private key is kept secret and never transmitted over an open network. The private key is used to decode data that has been encrypted with a user's public key, which is available to everyone over a network. In this way, a person can send information encrypted with Ron's public key, safe in the knowledge that only the holder of Ron's private key will be able to read it.

Prompt—On screen symbol that tells the user that the computer is ready to accept information or requests.

Proprietary—In general, something that is not used by everybody or that is specific to a certain company or agency. In the computer world, you may frequently hear programs or applets referred to as proprietary. i.e. proprietary e-mail, proprietary dialer.

Proprietary Dialer—A dialer that is used by a specific Internet provider or online service to connect to their system. Since it is proprietary, it will not work to connect any other ISP to the Internet besides the one that it is specifically designed for. Dial-up Networking is known as a standard dialer because it comes installed on all Windows machines (called Remote Access Service on Windows NT but virtually the same thing) and it is used by most standard ISPs. America Online is one service that has a proprietary dialer and does not use Dial-up Networking.

Public Key—The public part of a two-part encryption system. Users can encrypt information using someone's public key with the knowledge that only the owner of the corresponding private key will be able to open it. Conversely, users can encrypt information with their private keys so that the only way to read it is to decode it with the commonly available public key. This way, other users know for sure who sent data because only the correct public key will decode the information.

Push Technology—Personalized news and information from the Internet that can be delivered to you on a timely basis. One of the biggest buzzwords in the computer industry, a big advantage of push is that you can customize the news content that you receive to your liking. Whereas with newspaper technology, you get the whole thing—like it or not. The big names in push technology are PointCast, Marimba Castanet, and AirMedia Live. A lot of push client software displays information in a small window at the bottom of your screen. This small window is called a ticker. Some of these tickers include IBM News Ticker and My Yahoo! News Ticker. Sometimes, push takes the form of a screensaver that displays the latest news of your choice when the computer is idle. AfterDark Online and PointCast take the screensaver form of push.

Quick Launch Toolbar—**The little set of icons that are located between the Start button and the Taskbar. You can add things to this toolbar to make them easily accessible thus making it convenient to launch a program.**

Radio dials—The little hollow circles that you will find on some screens on the computer where a choice is required. You click inside the circle of the choice that you want, and it will put a little black dot inside the circle indicating your selection. They are called radio dials after the antiquated car radios that were around when 8-tracks were prevalent. The little knobs that had to be turned to change radio stations were called radio dials.

Random Access Memory—See RAM

RAM—Random Access Memory—Memory that is available to programs when the computer is running. When the computer is off, all information stored in the memory is lost.

Read Only Memory—See ROM

Read The Freaking Manual—See RTFM

Refresh Rate—The number of times per minute that a computer screen image is renewed.

Registry—The hierarchical program that controls the most rudimentary functions of Windows. It has the look of the Windows Explorer, but it essentially consists of 6 keys that control different functions of the system. The registry is composed of 2 files: user.dat and system.dat.

Removable Storage Media—Any drive that has a disk that can be removed easily. Essentially any drive that is not a fixed disk. Removable drives include floppy drives, Zip drives, CD-ROM drives, and Jazz drives.

Resolution—The amount of definition and clarity in an image on a monitor or from a printer. In monitors, resolution is measured by the number of pixels the device can display. In printers, resolution is measured in dots per inch (dpi) that can be printed on paper. Generally a user can dictate the number of pixels on a monitor, up to its capacity, by changing the display standards. In Windows, this capability is found in the Control Panel Display applet.

Restore Disk—A lot of computer manufacturers will include one of these in their software package. It provides an easy way to restore the computer back to the way it was when it was new. In other words, a restore disk will reinstall Windows and set all of the hardware configurations to factory default.

Ribbon Cable—Wide gray cable that attaches the internal drives of the computer to their controller cards.

ROM—Read Only Memory—Memory that is available to the computer only. Programs can not use it. ROM does not lose its information when the machine is turned off.

Root Directory—The mother of all directories. The root directory is the one from which all the other directories branch out; it has no parent directory. The root directory of a drive is the letter name of that drive followed by a backslash; for example, the root directory of the C: drive is the C:\DIRECTORY.

RTFM—Read The Freaking Manual—A techie acronym that is often used to allude to novice computer users that have a question that is answered in the computer manual.

Safe Mode—A diagnostic mode that a computer can sometimes be started in if it will not start normally. Safe Mode doesn't load any of the specific device drivers or anything that's not absolutely essential for Windows to boot. Frequently, when a computer won't start, it is due to a corrupt or conflicting driver and that is why Safe Mode is likely to start; it will not load that troublesome driver that is preventing the system from starting normally. Therefore, you can uninstall or change the driver that is keeping the computer from booting and then reboot in Normal Mode.

Scandisk—A Windows diagnostic program that is built into the operating system that scans the drive for errors and usually has the ability to self-fix them.

Screensaver—An animated picture or graphic that can be programmed through the Display control panel to come on the computer screen after so much inactivity time has elapsed. The main reason for a screensaver is to reduce wear and tear on the CRT (Cathode Ray Tube) inside the monitor that can burn out or become etched if the same window is left on for extended periods of time.

SCSI—Small Computer System Interface (Pronounced scuz-zee)—A standard for parallel interfaces that transfers information at a rate of up to 80MBps (megabytes per second). Up to seven peripheral devices, such as a hard drive and CD-ROM drive, can attach to a single SCSI port on the system's bus. SCSI ports were designed for Apple Macintosh and Unix Computers, but also can be used with properly equipped PCs.

SCSI ID—Number assigned to a SCSI device to set it apart from the other SCSI devices in the computer. The SCSI controller is usually seven and the boot hard drive is usually zero.

Search Engine—Software that searches through a database (a large cache of information) located on your computer. At Web-based search engines, users type a keyword query (descriptor words), and the search engine responds with a list of all sites in its database fitting the query description.

Secure Socket Layer—See SSL

Serial—A type of port that is usually used for the mouse and other external components such as a scanner. Serial ports transmit data one bit at a time.

Serial Line Internet Protocol—See SLIP

Server—A computer that is dedicated to a specific purpose such as a mail server or Web server. A server can actually be dedicated or non-dedicated. The latter is when a computer is used as a server of some sort and used for basic personal computing.

Shareware—Copyrighted software distributed on a time-restricted trial basis either via the Internet or by being passed along by satisfied customers.

Shorthand—In Internet lingo, these are really acronyms that are used in chat rooms and in newsgroups frequently to help abbreviate the conversation or message. An example of Internet shorthand is IIRC—If I remember correctly.

Signature File—A block signature that you can program your e-mail client to insert into every e-mail that you send out. It may include your real name or even a graphic of some sort that represents you or your company; these things will normally appear at the bottom of all of the e-mail that you send out once it is programmed into your mail program.

SIMM—See Single In-Line Memory Module

Simple Mail Transfer Protocol—See SMTP

Single In-Line Memory Module—A slender circuit board dedicated to storing memory chips. The chips are random access memory (RAM) upgrade chips used to expand the system's RAM capacity.

SLIP—Serial Line Internet Protocol—An Internet protocol that lets users gain 'Net access with a modem and a phone line. SLIP lets users link directly to the 'Net through an Internet service provider (ISP). It is slowly being replaced with its successor, Point-To-Point Protocol (PPP).

Small Computer System Interface—See SCSI

SMTP—Simple Mail Transfer Protocol—A mail server that handles the flow of all outgoing mail.

Smiley—Also referred to as emoticons. These are symbols that are used to portray moods or emotions. For example, ;-) is a winking smiley face. You may have to tilt your head sideways to recognize it. Smileys are usually used in chat rooms, e-mail, or instant messages to portray an entire mood or idea in just a symbol or combination of symbols. The stock smiley (J) can denote humor or sarcasm depending on the context in which it is used. See the long list of emoticons in the Appendix.

Snail Mail—Conventional mail handled by the United States Post Office. Snail mail was dubbed after e-mail was invented since electronic mail is so much faster.

Soft Modem—A modem that requires software to operate; usually these modems do not have their own processor, requiring the processing power of the CPU. As a result, soft modems use more computer resources than hard modems, but they are less expensive.

Soft Power Button—A power button to shut down or start a computer that can be programmed to have a delay of so many seconds. For instance, you can program the computer to require that the power button be held in for 5 seconds for the computer to be started or shut down.

Software—A set of instructions that can be executed on a computer to perform a specific function or functions.

Sound Card—An expansion card that adds audio capability beyond basic beeps.

SSL—Secure Socket Layer—A method of securing the transmission of confidential data through the Internet.

Standalone Computer—A computer that is not networked or directly linked with other computers.

Start Menu—The menu that ensues after clicking on the Start button; it can be invoked by pressing CTRL+ESC simultaneously.

Start Up Group—Applications that are programmed to load up and run in the background as soon as the computer is started. They are contained in a folder called Start Menu that is in the Windows directory; you can view all of these start up programs by looking at the list in the Close Program window.

Streaming Audio—An audio format experienced in real-time—users hear the audio file as it is downloaded without waiting for it to be completely downloaded.

Streaming Video—Technology that allows a user to see the contents of a video file as it is downloaded without waiting for the entire content of the file to be downloaded.

SuperDisk—A removable storage medium that resembles a floppy drive, but it has a much higher capacity or 120MB.

SVGA—Super Video Graphics Array—

Switch—A parameter added to a DOS command to modify or specialize it. This is done by adding a forward slash after the command and proceeded by the switch. For example, a "/h" switch will usually give help on how to use the command.

System—1 Applet in the control panel where you can access the Device Manager where all of the installed hardware is listed. 2 The computer itself as a whole.

System Administrator—Someone that is responsible for the configuration, maintenance, and security of a network. A Sys Admin Usually works in a corporate LAN environment.

System Resources—Defines how efficiently the computer is using the memory that it has available. The resources are expressed as a percentage and can be seen in My Computer by clicking Help then About Windows.

Systray—System Tray—The little section where the system clock sits usually in the lower-right corner of the Desktop. Sometimes, there will be a little megaphone on the Systray that you can use to adjust the speaker volume.

T1—A type of data connection able to transmit a digital signal at 1.544 megabits per second. T1 lines often are used to link large computer networks together, such as those that make up the Internet.

T3—A type of data connection able to transmit a digital signal at 44.746 megabits per second. Since this is about 40 times faster than T1 lines, large corporations, particularly computer or communications-type companies, will typically be networked with a T3 connection.

Tagram—The Tagram is what controls the speed enhancing feature of the computer, the cache memory.

TAPI—Telephone Application Programmers Interface—

Taskbar—Located between the Start button and the System Tray, the Taskbar will contain a rectangular icon for each program that is currently running at the time. If there are a lot of programs on the Taskbar, the icons will look more square and almost like they are stacked on top of one another.

TCP/IP—Transmission Control Protocol/Internet Protocol—A protocol governing communication among all computers on the Internet. It dictates how packets of information are sent over networks and ensures the reliability of data transmissions across Internet-connected networks.

TCP/IP Stack—Needed to properly use the TCP/IP protocol. A stack consists of TCP/IP software, sockets software (wsock.dll in Windows machines), and hardware drivers called packet drivers. Windows operating systems come with a TCP/IP stack built in including the wsock32.dll file.

Telephony—Technology that lets users use a PC to make and receive telephone calls. Telephony software often includes features such as voice mail, fax, auto dialing, and on-screen messaging.

Template—A ready-to-use, permanent document setup with basic layout, formatting commands, and formulas. Users can enter information to create individualized reports, letters and other documents.

Temporary Internet Files—A folder in the Windows directory that contains the text and graphics of every Web site that you have visited with Microsoft Internet Explorer.

Terabyte—1000 gigabytes or 1 trillion bytes.

Third-Party Programs—So called because these are applications that are not manufactured by your ISP or computer manufacturer, thus they belong to a 3rd party software maker. It could refer to an application that is not made by your company or the computer manufacturer or any similar circumstance.

Thumbnail—This is a miniature icon that represents a graphic and the icon is the graphic itself. In Windows Explorer, you can set the icons to be displayed as thumbnails by clicking View then Thumbnails.

TIFF—Tagged Image File Format (Pronounced *tiff*)—A common way to store bit-mapped graphic images on both PCs and Macintosh computers. TIFF is a platform-independent format, which means a TIFF image created on a PC can be viewed on a Macintosh, and vice versa. Bit-map files, on the other hand, are a graphic format for the Windows environment. This format was specifically designed for scanned images and is commonly used for that purpose. It can also be used in some applications to save images created on a computer. TIFF graphics can be color, grayscale, or black and white. The file extension for TIFF images is .tif.

Toolbar—Bar that is at the top of many windows on your computer. It lies beneath the Menu Bar and usually consists of a series of icons each offering different options or functions when clicked on.

Tower Unit—The box that houses all of the computer components.

Trace Route—A helpful Windows DOS command that will tell you the hops that a signal takes between server A and server B on the Internet and every server in between the 2 points that the signal may pass through.

Transmission Control Protocol/Internet Protocol—See **TCP/IP**

Trojan Horse—A program that is usually disguised as something fun or attractive like a graphic or screensaver, but that is really similar to a virus. Typically, A trojan horse program will not do any severe damage to your computer, unlike a virus, but it will do annoying things that are similar to a practical joke. For example, a trojan may make your computer not shut down when you choose to do so, or it may make your screen freeze when you sign onto your ISP. When the trojan is abolished, your computer will usually go back to working normally without having to reinstall Windows or something of that nature. A trojan carries within itself a means to allow the program's creator access to the system using it.

Universal Resource Locator—See **URL**

UNIX—Computer operating system that is designed to be used by many people at the same time. It is the most common operating system for servers on the Internet and it has TCP/IP integrated into it.

Update—To replace older versions of software or files with a newer version. Also refers to when a company releases a new version of software that's already on the market. This is usually indicated by a change in the version number, such as changing from 6.2 to 6.21. These software updates usually fix minor problems, or bugs, the older version contained.

Upload—To send or transmit a file from one computer to another via modem.

URL—Universal Resource Locator—In short, an Internet address. A standardized naming or addressing system for documents and media accessible over the Internet. For example, http://www.microsoft.com includes the type of document {a Hypertext Transfer Protocol [HTTP] document}, and the address of the computer on which it can be found {www.microsoft.com}.

Usenet—More commonly known as newsgroups. There are thousands of groups hosted on hundreds of servers around the world, dealing with nearly any topic imaginable. Newsreader software is required to download and view articles in the groups; the software generally uses the NNTP protocol. However, you can normally post an article to a group via e-mail.

UUencoding—Unix to Unix Encoding—A method for converting files from Binary to ASCII (text) so that they can be sent across the Internet via e-mail.

UUNET—The "Bulletin board of the Internet." Contains a collection of more than 20,000 discussion forums called newsgroups.

Veronica—Searches Gopher sites for file names and directories and consists of index server and search tool.

VESA—Video Electronics Standard Association—Newer protocol that supercedes VGA (Video Graphics Array) and SVGA (Super Video Graphics Array). It offers more support for new video cards available today that have a lot of RAM memory and can offer close to true-to-life 3d-rendering.

VGA—Video Graphics Array—

Video Capture Card—A special type of video card that is needed to perform certain functions such as to transfer an image from a video camera to your computer screen. There are All-In-Wonder video cards that serve as a video card, video capture card, and they can do such things as enable you to have your TV programs on the computer screen as a picture-in-picture.

Video Card—Hardware that controls how graphics are rendered on your computer monitor screen.

Virtual Memory—A type of hard drive space that mimics actual memory (RAM). When actual memory space is limited, the use of virtual memory can let users work with larger documents and run more software at once.

Virtual Private Networking—VPN—A protocol that can be installed in the Add/Remove Programs applet in the Control Panel (Add/Remove>Windows Setup>Communications). It enables a user to connect directory to another computer via the Dial-up Networking program and the data transmission is encrypted thus making it private.

Virus—A nasty program that is designed to harm your computer in some way. Some are nothing more than annoying pranks, and others can destroy the information on the hard drive or permanently damage internal components. Watch out and protect yourself from them using Anti-Virus software.

W3—World Wide Web Consortium—Organization that is responsible for establishing standard protocols on the WWW. More can be learned about the W3 by visiting their Web site at www.w3.org.

WAIS—Wide Area Information Server—A Unix-based system linked to the Internet or a program that allows users to search worldwide archives for resources based on a series of key words. Also called a Search Engine and it often times generates a list of documents that contain many "false drops" (irrelevant documents that don't really pertain to the search subject).

Warm Boot—The process of resetting the system by pressing Ctrl+Alt+Del at the same time.

Watermark—A feature in some digital cameras that automatically adds the date, time, text, graphics, borders, or other information to images.

Web—SEE WORLD WIDE WEB

Web Browser—Software that gives access to and navigation of the World Wide Web. Using a graphical interface that lets users click buttons, icons, and menu options to access commands, browsers show Web pages as graphical or text-based documents. Browsers allow users to download pages at different sites either by clicking hyperlinks (graphics or text presented in a different color than the rest of a document, which contains a programming code that connects to another page), or by entering a Web page's address, called a universal resource locator (URL).

Web Client—Synonym for Web browser.

Web Page—A document written in Hypertext Markup Language (HTML) that can be accessed on the Internet. Web pages are found by addresses called universal resource locators (URLs). Web pages can contain information, graphics, and hyperlinks to other Web pages and files.

Web Server—A computer on which a Web page resides. A server may be dedicated, meaning its sole purpose is to be the server, or non-dedicated, meaning it can be used for basic computing in addition to acting as the server. Good performance from a Web server, especially for busy sites, is crucial.

Wide Area Information Server—See WAIS

Windows Explorer—Screen that can be accessed in Windows 95 and above where you can view all of the files installed on the hard drive, or any drive for that matter, in a convenient hierarchical view. This is not to be confused with Internet Explorer, a Web browser made by Microsoft.

Wingdings—A type of font where each letter and number that you press on the keyboard will produce a symbol of some sort such as with the Wingdings2 font, typing the number 4 will produce a 4. There are different versions of the Wingdings font such as Wingdings1, Wingdings2, and Wingdings3; each version will have a different set of symbols associated with it.

WinZip—Application that is available on the Web site www.winzip.com. It is capable of unzipping (decompressing) or zipping (compressing) files.

Windows 3.x—Version of Windows that preceded Windows 95. Windows 3.x stands for Windows 3.1 and Windows 3.1.1—Windows for Workgroups—which contained support for networking that Windows 3.1 lacked. While Windows 3.x did have a GUI, it isn't, by definition, an operating system; it is really a Graphical User Interface that overlays DOS (Disk Operating System).

Windows 95—Major upgrade from Windows 3.x and the first genuine operating system for an IBM based machine. The entire look and feel was changed in this Window version over Windows 3.x, and the navigational menus and screens were almost completely different. The Program Manager in 3.x became the Desktop; the File Manager became the Windows Explorer, for example.

Windows NT 4.0—Similar on the surface to Window 95. The bare bones of NT is much different than Windows 95, however. Not actually an upgrade to Window 95, but it is sometimes considered one. It is geared towards a network environment such as a corporate LAN. Windows NT is not as user-friendly as Windows 95, and the 2 operating systems are really best used for their intended purposes. Windows 95 is a better choice for a computer novice or someone that mainly just uses the PC to send e-mail, go to the Web, and do basic tasks such as Word Processing. Windows NT is the best choice for a computer professional or someone that is very computer literate; it is known for it's increased security over Windows 95 meaning that it would be the best choice for a network—especially where security is a concern.

Windows 98—Direct upgrade from Window 95. Although it is considered a major upgrade, it is not nearly as drastic of a change as from Windows 3.x to Windows 95. Windows 98 appears a lot like Windows 95, but it has many enhancements hidden under its skin. Windows 98 has increased driver support for a lot more hardware than Windows 95 offers; it has increased networking support over Windows 95 as well. Windows 98 has an incremental upgrade called Windows 98 Second Edition; it is a minor upgrade in comparison to the other Windows upgrades, but it has Microsoft Internet Explorer 5.0 integrated into the operating system and it has even more networking support than Windows 98 as well as more multimedia capabilities.

Windows Millennium Edition—Major upgrade from Windows 98 that is the biggest technological advancement to the Windows operating system since the jump from Windows 3.x to Windows 95. It is much more stable than Windows 98, and it has very good unprecedented multimedia capabilities. It does appear similar to Windows 98, but many of the menus, icons, and drop-down lists changed in Windows Millenium. In short, it is a good fully featured stable OS that has many improvements over Windows 98. It's user-friendliness and networking capabilities makes it a wise choice for a computer novice and an expert alike.

Windows 2000 Professional—Windows NT based operating system that is really a direct upgrade path from Windows NT 4.0 Workstation. Like Windows NT, this operating system is best suited to a computer expert or system administrator and computer novices should shy away from this OS unless they have a specific reason for using it.

Winsocks—**1** Stands for Windows Sockets. Winsocks is a set of protocols that programmers use for creating TCP/IP applications for use with Windows. **2** Part of the TCP/IP stack that is necessary to use the TCP/IP protocol. In laymen's terms, a file called wsock32.dll is necessary on a Windows machine to make a connection to the Internet. The wsock32.dll file should be located in the C:\Windows\System directory; it should be 65kb in Windows 95, 40kb in Windows 98, and 36kb in Windows Me.

Wordpad—Word processor that is built into Windows 95 and every subsequent version of Windows. Prior to Windows 95, the rudimentary version of the Wordpad program was called Write. It is a rather simple word processor that is more sophisticated than Notepad but simpler than a full-fledged word processor such as Microsoft Word.

World Wide Web—The portion of the Internet that has become the most popular and consists of millions of Web pages that are joined together by hyperlinks.

World Wide Web Consortium—SEE W3

Worm—A computer program that replicates itself and is self-propagating. The main difference between a worm and a virus is that viruses are intended to cause problems on standalone machines and attack boot sectors and files on the hard disk. Worms are specifically designed to permeate network environments. The most notorious worm was the Internet Worm of November 1988. It propagated itself on over 6,000 systems across the Internet.

Zip Drive—A removable storage media kind of like a Jazz drive, but its disks don't hold as much information. However, Zip drives are in much greater use than Jazz drives probably due to the higher cost of Jazz drives and the disks that are needed for them.

Zip File—A file that has been compressed usually to expedite its transfer over the Internet in e-mail. It is necessary to have software that is capable of unzipping or decompressing a zip file. The most popular program that will unzip files is WinZip.

Bibliography

1 Sweet, Lisa L. *Internet Computing Magazine* "Seeking Windows Compatibility," Volume 3 Issue 6. (chapter 5)

2 Spector, Lincoln *PC World* "Free Support Free-for-All" pgs. 139-146 *The best and the worst technical support study* p. 141 (chapter 6)

3 Scalet, Sarah D. *Pc Novice* GUIDE TO *Internet Basics* **"Your First Time Online—** What to Expect When You're On The 'Net," Volume 6 Issue 10 pgs 52-54. (chapter 8)

4 Carberry, Sonya *Smart Computing in plain English Windows Tips & Tricks Superguide* **"Windows File Systems**—*What You Need To Know About FAT16, FAT32 & NTFS, "*
Volume 6 Issue 6 pg. 62-64.
(chapter 12)

Index

_____E_____

F

I

J-K-L

_____N-O_____

_____P_____

R

___T-U-V___

___X-Y-Z___

www.ingramcontent.com/pod-product-compliance
Lightning Source LLC
Chambersburg PA
CBHW051224050326

40689CB00007B/789